Taking Forward the

Primary Curriculum

Applying the 2014 National Curriculum for KS1 and KS2

Edited by Roy Blatchford

A John Catt Publication

First Published 2013

by John Catt Educational Ltd,
12 Deben Mill Business Centre, Old Maltings Approach,
Melton, Woodbridge IP12 1BL

Tel: +44 (0) 1394 389850 Fax: +44 (0) 1394 386893
Email: enquiries@johncatt.com
Website: www.johncatt.com

ISBN: 978 1 908095 95 4

Set and designed by John Catt Educational Limited

Printed and bound in Great Britain
by Cambrian Printers

Contents

Taking Forward the Primary Curriculum

About the contributors

Kate Atkins has been teaching in Lambeth for nearly 20 years. She is an early years expert and has worked at Rosendale Primary School, a three-form entry school with a Children's Centre, for nine years, the last two as Head of School. The school bursts with innovation: housing its library in a double decker London bus; broadcasting a weekly radio show; and developing a system of learning that sees children assessing their own learning and publishing to a world-wide audience.

Roy Blatchford is Director of the National Education Trust (www. nationaleducationtrust.net) in England, formerly a Headteacher and one of Her Majesty's Inspectors of Schools (HMI). He has served as education adviser to successive UK governments and had held education briefs in the UAE, India, the USA and Thailand. He is the author/editor of over 150 books, including *Sparkling Classrooms, Different Cultures, Reflected Values and The Restless School*.

Tim Coulson has taught in London primary schools and was Headteacher of William Tyndale Primary School in Islington. He has worked for national and local government in a number of roles, including as National Director of the National Numeracy Strategy. He has since 2012 been Director of Education for Essex County Council.

Kate Dethridge leads Churchend Primary Academy and has completed 15 years in this Headship. The school has twice been graded 'Outstanding' by Ofsted and the school is a National Support School. Kate has been a National Leader of Education for six years and was awarded a Fellowship with the National College in 2009. Kate is an Ofsted inspector and was a member of Lord Bew's panel that reviewed Key Stage 2 Assessment & Testing in 2011.

Professor Deborah Eyre is Education Director at Nord Anglia Education, a premium international schools organisation. Working with governments and schools across the world on issues around educational quality and advanced cognitive performance she is a leading figure in gifted education. Deborah was formerly the Director of the National Academy for Gifted and Talented Youth and an academic at the universities of Warwick and Oxford Brookes.

Kate Frood has taught in inner London for 30 years, almost entirely in the borough of Camden. She is currently ten years into her second Headship, at Eleanor Palmer School. Kate has (accidentally) developed a reputation for primary mathematics and teaches problem-solving to Years 5 and 6 every week. Eleanor Palmer recently became a National Teaching School.

Dr Neil Hawkes is known internationally for his focus on values-based education. His engaging philosophy and practice can now be seen in numerous countries. For instance, Australia has embraced many of Neil's ideas as have Sweden, Holland, Iceland, Norway, New Zealand, Ireland and the UK. He is Founder of the International Values Education Trust, and his latest publication *From My Heart* has been widely acclaimed.

Richard Howard is Chair of the National Education Trust, an independent charitable foundation leading and promoting excellent practice and innovation in education. Following two primary Headships, he was Chief Education Adviser in Oxfordshire, and has extensive national experience in education, including the development of state/independent schools' partnerships. He is an Honorary Fellow of Oxford Brookes University.

Peter Hyman is Headteacher and one of the founders of School 21, a new 4-18 school in Stratford, East London. He is the author of *1 Out Of 10: From Downing Street Vision To Classroom Reality*.

Pamela Matty has been Head of Grove Primary School in Handsworth, Birmingham for 16 years. Previously she led the mathematics advisory team in Birmingham, developing extended training programmes with the Open University, and promoting city-wide events to raise the profile of maths education. Pamela has written a wide range of articles and materials for Scholastic Education and other publishers. She is an accredited Ofsted inspector.

Chris Nourse has been a primary Headteacher for ten years and currently leads Somerford Community Primary School, situated in an area of social deprivation in Christchurch, Dorset. He has recently returned from the Middle East where he was the founding Principal of an international primary school. Prior to this Chris led the amalgamation of an infant and junior School in Surrey, opened a children's centre, and chaired a confederation of 16 schools and settings.

Katy Peters is the Principal of Battle Primary Academy in Reading, the National Education Trust's first sponsored academy. Having been a class teacher and music specialist for ten years she has been in post as the leader of this diverse school for two years, taking it out of special measures and working towards becoming an 'Outstanding' academy.

Laurence Pitt has worked at Ashley Down in Bristol for 10 years. The school has grown from a 240 place junior school to a split-site, 840-place primary school federation over that time. He is a National Leader of Education; Ashley Down is a National Support School and a National Teaching School.

Will Power teaches Year 6 in an East London school where he is also Science subject leader. He is an alumnus of the Teach First Leadership Development Programme and is currently studying for an MA in Educational Leadership. Before teaching, Will worked for a rural development NGO in Jharkhand,

India, developing a model for low cost, high quality schools. He continues to work as an Associate of Adhyayan, a Mumbai-based education consultancy.

Jane Ratcliffe is Headteacher of St John's Primary School in Wallingford, Oxfordshire. She has been in post since 2010, and has worked in senior leadership and advisory roles in Oxfordshire for 15 years. Under her leadership, the school has been transformed into an innovative and creative place where independence and collaboration are at the centre of the inspiring curriculum. She has recently established an academy trust with neighbouring primary schools.

Dave Smith has been a primary Headteacher for 13 years and currently leads Longlevens Junior, a four-form entry school on the outskirts of Gloucester with an outstanding creative arts profile. He has also served as LA associate adviser and primary strategy consultant leader. In recent years, Dave's position as a Headteacher has been combined with system leadership and curriculum development roles with the National College.

Rob Stokoe is Director of Jumeirah English Speaking Schools, Dubai, with 25 years leadership experience including primary, secondary and a five-year spell with the University of Sunderland. He has had the privilege of working alongside many gifted and dedicated educationalists, adding in inspection and evaluation work with Ofsted, the International Baccalaureate and the government authorities within Dubai and the UAE.

Kathy Wood has successful experience as a teacher, Headteacher, Ofsted inspector working in the UK and overseas, and as an external examiner for teacher training programmes. For six years she worked regularly as a consultant and leader of education reform projects for UNICEF in Eastern Europe. Since 2004 she has been Headteacher of Hornbill School, Brunei, a school serving MoD personnel. In 2007 she received an MBE for services to education and MoD.

Chris Yapp has 30 years experience in the IT industry, with over 20 years interest in IT and learning. He writes, blogs and consults around technology futures and their social and economic impacts. He wrote and co-edited *Personalizing Learning in the 21st Century*. He is a patron of NACE.

Foreword

This book has a simple intent. In September 2014, primary schools in England will be expected to adopt a new national curriculum. There is good time to prepare.

At this point of curriculum change and development in England's schools, the contributors offer their considered reflections on how primary schools across the country might take forward and shape their own curriculum framework for pupils. The spirit of the book is, based on considerable leadership experience in schools, letting-a-thousand-flowers-bloom rather than recommending a one-size-fits-all approach.

This book does not set out to analyse the content of the 2014 Primary Curriculum, nor to present ways in which individual schools should plan their schemes of work and weekly or monthly planning. That is rightly the province of each school, learning from and sharing best practice with others.

Rather, the contributors to this book present underpinning values, ideas and approaches to successful curriculum planning, rooted in many years of leading and working in schools. Their reflections come from varying perspectives: teachers, Headteachers, directors of foundations and leading thinkers on education, each of whom is involved in the work of the National Education Trust (www.nationaleducationtrust.net), an independent charitable foundation which champions best practice.

Part A: National and international perspectives begins with an historical account from Richard Howard, Chair of the National Education Trust. He also draws attention to the vital importance of listening to the children's voice when reviewing the school curriculum.

Deborah Eyre, Rob Stokoe, Chris Nourse and Kathy Wood offer their distinctive perspectives from different parts of the world; what they have to say presents some common themes and not a few challenges to the status quo.

Tim Coulson and Neil Hawkes focus their chapters on children's dispositions and attitudes, and the importance of all schools, within their local communities, adopting a *values-added* approach to the curriculum alongside the important value-added measurement.

Chris Yapp is a renowned writer on technology and is not shy of challenging the teaching profession to think differently. My own Chapter 9 reminds schools that they have considerable flexibilities: considering what the national curriculum stipulates *should* be taught, while at the same time determining their own distinct school curriculum.

Part B: Implementing the new curriculum opens with Peter Hyman's strong plea to look afresh at the curriculum, from 4 to 18, followed by Will Powers's complementary account of his classroom experiences and the need to look at learning from a child's perspective.

As Headteachers in different contexts, Kate Atkins and Jane Ratcliffe present powerful, perhaps radical ideas on the subject of independent learning, while Dave Smith, Katy Peters and Laurence Pitt bring their own different leadership experiences to innovative curriculum design, including reference to the critical role of early years education.

Also writing as Headteachers, Kate Frood, Pamela Matty and Kate Dethridge set out clearly the importance of the core skills of literacy and numeracy being at the heart of the curriculum, but never to the exclusion of excitement and fresh ideas for children.

****

A few notes on the 2014 Primary Curriculum

1. Key Stages 1 and 2 remain as two phases across which the curriculum is structured.

2. Programmes of study and attainment targets remain in the vocabulary of planning.

3. Core and foundation subjects (Figure 1 below) similarly remain as a way of grouping subjects.

Figure 1 – Structure of the national curriculum

	Key stage 1	Key stage 2	Key stage 3	Key stage 4
Age	5 – 7	7 – 11	11 – 14	14 – 16
Year groups	1 – 2	3 – 6	7 – 9	10 – 11
Core subjects				
English	✓	✓	✓	✓
Mathematics	✓	✓	✓	✓
Science	✓	✓	✓	✓
Foundation subjects				
Art and design	✓	✓	✓	
Citizenship			✓	✓
Computing	✓	✓	✓	✓
Design and technology	✓	✓	✓	
Languages[1]		✓	✓	
Geography	✓	✓	✓	
History	✓	✓	✓	
Music	✓	✓	✓	
Physical education	✓	✓	✓	✓

Figure 2 – Statutory teaching of religious education and sex and relationship education

	Key stage 1	Key stage 2	Key stage 3	Key stage 4
Age	5 – 7	7 – 11	11 – 14	14 – 16
Year groups	1 – 2	3 – 6	7 – 9	10 – 11
Religious education	✓	✓	✓	✓
Sex and relationship education			✓	✓

4. Strong cross-curricular themes are:

- Inclusion
- High expectations of every pupil
- Numeracy and mathematics
- Language and literacy

5. The weighting of the 2014 curriculum – just measured in pages allocated per subject – is strongly towards English and mathematics

6. An assessment regime is not stipulated, with schools free to continue using the current National Curriculum Levels or evolve new systems.

****

So, there is both continuity and change in curriculum content. There are great opportunities to build on current successful practices and shape the future. As someone who visits hundreds of primary classrooms every year, I can assert with confidence that the education of our nation's children is in safe and wise hands. During this period of curriculum evolution every primary Headteacher and teacher will think carefully about change that has as its proper focus their pupils' good learning and outcomes.

As a team of writers who are enthusiastic about the importance and power of primary education, we hope what you read here motivates, challenges and even inspires you to bring further memorable learning to the nation's classrooms.

Roy Blatchford
Oxford 2013

Part A

National and international perspectives

Chapter 1

Who owns the school curriculum now?

Richard Howard

In his latest book (1), the author David Winkley describes his first teaching appointment in a junior school run by an eccentric and supremely autocratic Headteacher, Mr Worsley. Despite this despot's rejection of any aspect of the curriculum that might involve imagination or creativity, he would address – often at little notice, despite full attendance being demanded – the hastily assembled staff with his views on the future of education.

> *"Mark my words, staff, we can expect terrible shifts in the balance of power. Governments will suddenly begin to notice us and despise all that we are trying to do… and then they'll begin to think they can manage schools themselves from Westminster. We can expect an army of intruders and do-gooders – mark my words – under an ocean of papers, we shall drown. Tormented by an army of inquisitors, we shall be crushed under foot. And we shall be weaponless. Exposed and naked to the winds."*

Mr Worsley reminds me a bit about Emrys Davies, President of the NUT in the early 1960s, and a primary school Headteacher. He was distinguished by his practice of standing for a few minutes each day in his school hall which was surrounded by all of the ten classrooms; normally he then retired to his office except if he heard a noise from any of the classrooms in which case he would knock at the door, enter and then utter his usual comment – 'all well in here. Miss Jones?' Nothing further was needed to ensure that he could, again, retire to his office.

The Headteacher, in those days, held an almost unassailable position and could, if he or she wished, completely command order within the school without really considering new ideas. But new ideas have always been with us; there have always been those who, as now, have pioneered what might improve learning, what might make a better deal for learning.

What is and what might be

A few years before Mr Worsley's time, working with and encouraging emerging groups of school leaders in the mid 1950s, who were themselves to presage the Plowden Report, the former HMI and teacher Christian Schiller had spoken with greater, and perhaps more considered, perspicacity about what was likely to happen in schools.

He was concerned about the obsession with regarding learning as a series of school subjects in defining the curriculum. He lectured with an apparent freedom but his thinking came from careful observation of children in schools, especially those skills in which they were already and naturally confident and those so-called skills which were being forced upon them by the needs of the 'curriculum'. In one of those lectures, he said:

> *"Curriculum – the word itself has a Latin derivation, arising from chariot racing in the Roman Games; ferociously competitive; circular in direction and with ever deepening tracks where a number of such vehicles were certain to founder..."*

Longer ago – now more than a hundred years – Edmund Holmes was saying something similar. E.G.A. Holmes was an HMI in the 1890s and the early years of the twentieth century. I think I know, even now, that he was a diligent and deeply committed inspector, concerned about what constituted good learning and how young people might best be encouraged to learn. That I feel I know this about him is that, written in the Headteacher's hand in a moulding logbook in the village school where I was once the Headteacher, were his reports of visit – and I read through all the entries in these logs, written as they were in a beautiful and carefully constrained hand.

There are reports on the school in 1907 and 1910 which Holmes had visited, and sent to the Headteacher within a couple of days for him to copy into the logbook. On each occasion, Holmes had arrived at the school at an early hour in a pony and trap from the city station some ten miles away and then spent the day 'examining the pupils'. He inspected the needlework of the 'babies class', listened to recitations, scrutinised the handwriting, observed arithmetic and grammar drills. He also inspected the earth closets and the drains and considered the degree to which the roof leaked above the main classroom.

Somehow, his reports sought to convey positive aspects of the school whilst alerting the 'Managers' to the roof leaks and the need to increase the coal allowance for the Headteacher and his wife, the mistress of the babies class, as well as indicating that the alphabet would be better taught by the purchase of a new manual which would cost 1s and 6d.

Despite his commitment and attention to detail and the way in which his concern for continuous improvement was always tellingly expressed, Holmes found his inspection work stultifying. He felt he needed to set out his concerns about overly prescriptive requirements for what children should learn and how they should be judged to be proficient as learners. When he retired, he published a book in 1913, *What Is And What Might Be*. His words, written a century ago do not, really, seem to be merely historical:

> *"For a third of a century "My Lords at the Board of Education" required their inspectors to examine every child in every elementary school in England on a syllabus which was binding on all schools alike. In doing this, they put a bit*

into the mouth of the teacher and drove him, at their pleasure, in this direction and that. And what they did to him they compelled him to do to the child. "

Visionary statements were made in the Hadow Report over 70 years ago that the curriculum should be *'thought of in terms of activity and experience, rather than of knowledge to be acquired and facts to be stored'*. And in 1967 the Plowden Report stated boldly: *'One of the main educational tasks of the primary school is to build on and strengthen children's intrinsic interest in learning and lead them to learn for themselves rather than from fear of disapproval or desire for praise.'*

Yet the words of Holmes seem more appropriate than those of Hadow or Plowden in terms of expressing current practices across our nation's primary schools.

The secret garden

Holmes was referring to the Payment by Results scheme introduced in 1863 whereby schools were funded in part dependent upon on the outcome of exams conducted by school inspectors. The scheme was abandoned in the 1890s as school managers were getting bogged down by the paperwork. Of course, contemporary comparisons are obvious. Recently, the hitherto non-militant National Association of Headteachers (NAHT) passed a vote of no-confidence in the Secretary of State and has considered school-based alternatives to the present Ofsted inspection procedures.

Antagonism to the holder of the Education portfolio in any government's cabinet is by no means new. In recent times, the lack of cohesive thought about what constitutes what Hadow stated in 1931 as: 'What a wise and good parent will desire for his own children, a nation must desire for all children' has been of contention between successive governments and academics and teachers since at least the 1980s.

It was then and there that the National Curriculum was devised. It was introduced in 1991 and has been revised ever since. There are now about 18% of the country's teaching force who were trained and started teaching before the National Curriculum. The fact that most teachers today have no concept of what went before – *ie* the time when teachers followed no central directives – has at least two outcomes.

For nearly a century – until the early 1990s – there was really no defined national framework for what schools should be doing. For good schools, this led to creative and inspired work and learning; it also allowed poor practice all-too-often to go unreported. In many ways the teaching profession failed to articulate clearly what it was the children and young people were learning and the extent to which they were making, or not making, progress. There remained, even as recently as 20 years ago, lines across the playground indicating that parents should pass no further.

17

Estelle Morris, recalling her early career at a 2013 National Education Trust seminar which she hosted, remembered that her teaching was never observed, except for a cursory glance during her 'probationary year'; and that she was never made aware of how the students were doing beyond her own subject. The lack of openness about the 'secret garden' created a vacuum of understanding about the nation's schools, and the politicians readily filled the gap to the extent that 24,000 schools could become centrally controlled from Westminster.

Only a few decades ago, the Ministry of Education wrote to schools no more than twice a year – at most – usually introducing the letter by the gentle and courteous phrase: information for the consideration of teachers. It was interesting that letters were addressed to Head Masters and Head Mistresses of Secondary Schools in capital letters and headteachers of primary schools in lower case – a hierarchy which of course has long disappeared! What has grown is now an almost daily set of requirements, criticisms and new plans from the centre, not always based on careful research or comparators.

The distinguished commentator on primary education John Coe wrote in 2013:

The unwise and unproductive pressure on children and their teachers to produce immediate results has had a major impact on school life. Unicef in 2007 found that in terms of children's wellbeing the UK ranked below the other 21 OECD countries studied. We were at the very bottom of the list. There has been a significant increase in the number of children suffering from conduct, behavioural and emotional problems and one in ten has a clinically diagnosed mental health issue. We have to face the fact that we are creating unhappiness and recognise that this has a direct impact on educational attainment since happy and fulfilled children learn most easily.

There is worry and anger in many schools that the professional voice is being ignored, that casual conversations are being used to indicate major trends and that antagonism to the work of schools is supplanting the necessary support and promotion of where there is good practice. No school leader worth his or her salt, is going to resent challenge. Indeed, all good leaders thrive on challenge and offer the same to those that they work with. They never 'walk past poor practice'; as Tim Brighouse once observed:

Leaders will regard crisis as the norm and complexity as fun. They will experience a lot of both.

Daring to be different

I've had the opportunity over the last few years of visiting the National Education Trust's Advocacy Schools (2). They are special places for learning; they are doing very well; they are relentless in pursuing the highest quality for their children and young people; they positively achieve and their community values them enormously. They also share that worry and anger about what is currently going on in the press, in government pronouncements and in Ofsted findings.

Something similar to this concern was happening in Ontario a few years ago and, just as our policy makers wish to do something about it, so those in that Canadian state decided to make changes. But they did it differently:

Ontario did not centrally script and cascade new teaching and learning practices to all classrooms. Instead, it focused on cultivating school-led innovation and improvement. As one Ontario system leader described, "We minimized the amount of directing or mandating we did. Instead, we needed methods to get school professionals' ideas so we could build on them. We regularly brought people together to share their practices and exchange ideas. We did almost no mandating of specific strategies – we got them to develop their own plans. We didn't micromanage schools or districts in this process". (3)

Probably Edmund Holmes or Christian Schiller would want to add voice to this statement if they could. Equally important to taking account of what the best school leaders are saying, is to do what they do and further take account of what the children are saying. When Jim Rose was undertaking his Curriculum Review some six years ago, the National Education Trust asked children from primary schools across the country to suggest how best the curriculum should be developed: a Children's Charter.

Among the things the children said were:

- We want to learn about real things, things which matter to us
- We want to break down barriers between subjects into real live topics
- We want to learn from experts who inspire us – artists, scientists, writers
- We want to learn more about the world, world events and where we live
- We want to be involved in what we learn – what interests and inspires us
- We want more opportunities to work in teams, to learn from one another and to work with different age groups.
- We want more time to learn, more time to research and more time to finish
- We want to learn by doing and making
- We want to learn with our parents and other adults
- We want to communicate our learning through the technologies we use
- We want to communicate (with) and learn from children in other countries
- We want to learn more by being outside the classroom and outside the school
- We want to be listened to.

There's an agenda for growth! It's easy to use some infantile statements – 'from the mouth of babes'; 'don't throw the baby out with bathwater'. But, of course, that is what we are in danger of doing. Let us encompass all the positive trends that Ontario found when it asked the teachers what worked best; let us take account of the fact that children are sophisticated in how they describe their expectations of education. Let us return to providing, even invigorating, some guarantees for all children during their fifteen years of provided schooling.

This following list might be a start, and there will be plenty of Headteachers who can properly add to these and correct my prejudices where they exist: it is for every child to have:

- the experience of a residential visit
- the opportunity to perform
- the challenge of preparing and completing a substantial piece of work – in writing; in art; in public speaking; in music or drama
- the challenge of improving on previous best
- the dignity of being literate and numerate.

Perhaps both sides of the present 'stand-off' between the national policy makers and those that lead and teach in schools might consider the text, written by a red hot poker on a piece of wood which then hung over the bed of Alec Clegg's aunt in Yorkshire:

> *'If of fortune thou be bereft,*
> *And of thine earthly store have left*
> *Two loaves, sell one and with the dole*
> *Buy hyacinths to feed the soul.'*

Clegg was an inspirational education officer and he, along with many teachers, found ways to inculcate and celebrate the elemental quality in children's writing and illustration. He believed that they could really tell how it was – and, of course, they did, and so tellingly. There is an abiding 'earthly store' and in so many schools the soul is being fed. It remains for all of those in schools to tell it as it happens just as in Ontario – it's a good story, really.

References

1. Mr Worsley, David Winkley (2013)
2. www.nationaleducationtrust.net
3. 'How the world's most improved schools keep on getting better', McKinsey (2010)

Wider reading

Nudge, Richard Thaler & Cass Sunstein

School Wars, Melissa Benn

The Learning Game, Jonathan Smith

Proust and the Squid, Maryannne Wolf

Chapter 2

International perspectives on the primary curriculum

Deborah Eyre

'Education is not the filling of a pail, but the lighting of a fire.' W.B. Yeats

Primary school education is subject to continual change and refinement not least because we are unclear as to what we think good primary education should look like and what it should achieve. Liberal education systems, such as that in the UK, build on a distinguished canon of philosophical thinking stretching from Mill to Wittgenstein and Dewey and have highly developed views on purpose and style.

For other countries the rationale for their education systems can be a little different and often include structural ideas such as universal education for all students regardless of gender, culture or background. Until this is secured, the question of say 'style' and philosophy of primary education may be seen by some as an unhelpful debate.

In South Sudan, for example, most adults haven't experienced primary education because of war and so finding teachers who can teach the next generation is an issue. Also, as in much of Africa, the text books being used are imported and not related to South Sudan's history or geography and so carving out an educational philosophy for South Sudan's primary education is a complex and multi-dimensional problem. Yet one might still argue that without a framework of philosophical intention, structures and operational delivery lack heart.

More developed countries such as Abu Dhabi, Qatar and Saudi Arabia are often looking to the education system as a mechanism to help their nationals 'catch-up' with aspects of western education, whilst China and the Far East have a distinguished tradition of education reaching back to Confucius which they are now reframing to ensure their education system positions students for the increased economic growth. So, Asia's strong philosophy continues to steer the nature of primary education while in the Middle East they are still struggling to align their traditional philosophies with their modernistic intentions.

But even in highly developed countries such as ours, educational theories in liberal tradition have themselves undergone a major transformation in recent years in response to changing demographics and technological developments. McDonough and Feinberg (2003) (1) talk of considering how best to redefine and reassert the core values of liberal democracy in the light of new circumstances and conflicts created by multicultural democracies. They are recognising a significant shift in education. A shift in thinking re the purposes of education, in the possibilities created by education and in the demands now placed upon education.

So all this leads to a lively and interesting debate about what primary education should be in the UK and the west, as well as in countries across the globe.

Interestingly, in most countries, regardless of their wealth or political complexion, the same broad themes are being discussed. This does not mean that the solutions are all the same – solutions are necessarily related to the individual context – but it does mean that international dialogue is fruitful and productive. These five themes, set out below, emerge as having relevance and importance in England as well as across the globe.

1. Knowledge versus process and skills: is it really an either/or?

'Excellence is not a skill. It is an attitude.' Ralph Marston

Worldwide this question of knowledge versus skills is high on the agenda for education policy makers. In the west there are those who suggest that in the age of rapid knowledge access via internet, *etc.* this preoccupation with securing knowledge is outdated. These proponents suggest that we need not knowledge but rather a curriculum that foregrounds the application of knowledge through a focus on problem solving.

Interestingly Hong Kong, China and Singapore – who all score highly in the knowledge and skills based OECD PISA assessments (2) – are now looking to help their students become better problem-solvers. Indeed they are looking to the West to help them. Asian education systems are traditionally strong on subject knowledge but arguably less good on the application of that knowledge. Policy makers have recognised this and are looking to address it. However, they are not looking to reduce the focus on knowledge acquisition. Indeed, high levels of subject knowledge are seen as crucial to being able to create innovative and effective solutions to problems. In short, without the relevant knowledge you cannot use it.

In the UK, universities make this same point in respect of some GCSE course content and the problem that creates for advanced study. Strong subject knowledge is the key to success. So only the most extreme are looking at a knowledge-free or knowledge-reduced curriculum. The best are looking at identifying an ambitious body of knowledge and the skills thought to be required to equip their students to operate in a sophisticated technological world, and then teaching through a more enquiry based approach. This enquiry based methodology becomes the mechanism for developing a problem solving mind-set and problem solving skills.

2. Back to basics: securing the 3 Rs

'So instead of watching TV, we read every night together as a family.' Arne Duncan

Securing the 3Rs is an educational goal for primary education worldwide and an indicator of a successful system. In some countries securing universal literacy is the major focus for primary education. Reading is seen as key to academic success and alongside numeracy is at the forefront of primary education. It is seen as a universal right for every child. All other aspects of primary education are seen as supplementary and primary education structures reflect this commitment.

So it is interesting for us to reflect on how we have reached a position where close to 20% of children leave our English primary schools without these skills. And we are not alone. Similar statistics relate to the USA. What are we doing wrong? The most common reasons cited for this relate to either the child's ability or family background. Of course we do know that parents can make a big difference to how their child performs at school but the international discussion is around 'are we just reaching for too easy an excuse?' It is unlikely that the countries that do better are populated by exemplary parents offering optimal support. Is it not, in part, the role of an education system to compensate children for inadequate parents rather than compound it?

Equally, all countries have children for whom learning comes easily and others for whom it does not. The best systems ensure that all children grasp the basics which will enable them to progress. They have no long tail of underachievement.

3. Technology: opportunity or distraction

'Technology tools such as laptops are the kind of help that we need. A program that provides laptops for all youngsters would close a gap that most of us are not aware of, or will not admit to, which is a tremendous gap in the poor communities.' Major Owens

Another global debate is the role of technology. In the late 1990s Lord Puttnam likened the advent of technology in school to the advent of the 'talkies' in cinema. It would redefine education. Well changes have occurred but not at the level Puttnam was anticipating.

Laptops, iPads and interactive whiteboards are being used to support existing pedagogy. In some countries, *eg* Hong Kong, IT is being used to reduce cost – putting the mandatory text books online so they can be updated regularly and at low cost. This is not radical pedagogy, it is the same material but downloadable. So technology is creating pragmatic, useful solutions but not the anticipated pedagogical step-change.

New thinking in technology is however causing discussion at an international level. The creation of MOOCs (3) where the world's universities are putting their course content online has triggered a debate about the value of everyone producing their own material. If the best content is freely available why not just produce it in the major languages and then consider how best to present it to children in individual contexts. The skill needed would then be around how to navigate or interact with the content. The teacher could set enquiry based tasks, or memory tasks or knowledge and comprehension tasks. Khan Academy (4) has led the way at the primary level and their material is being accessed by children in a wide variety of countries in a wide variety of ways.

Equally, debate exists around the use of discourse or discussion online and how it can enhance learning by connecting children from different locales to study in a group or team. Nord Anglia Education's virtual learning platform (Global Classroom) for its thirty schools across twelve countries enables students from seventy nationalities to discuss learning topics with experts on a daily basis. Who is your teacher and where they are located is being truly redefined in projects such as these all over the world, but have yet to make it to the mainstream of government delivered education.

4. Education for creating civilised citizens or tomorrow's workforce: ethics and values

'Formal education will make you a living; self-education will make you a fortune.' Jim Rohn

A vastly contested area in primary education relates to the main purposes of education. These debates are rarely as straightforward and clear cut as they might appear. Hence whilst concepts around sociology and economics purposes tend to be presented as polar opposites, in reality they are not. No country would seek to create good citizens who are unemployable or alternatively employees with no conscience or concern or others. So the nature of the discussion is around how much priority to give to each.

In Saudi Arabia, for example, whilst they are looking to create citizens who are employable their dominant concern is to ensure that they do so without losing their traditional values. In their view the West's preoccupation with 'self' has worrying implications for citizenship. It may produce children who are more concerned with what is happening to them then what is happening to others. Selfishness may dominate.

Obviously, countries like the Asian tiger countries who are candid in seeing education as the pipeline to talent in the workforce and hence economic success, do not wish to jettison their traditional values either. Nonetheless they foreground academic success more strongly and have been inclined to leave citizenship development more to the family.

In the West and in England we have yet to achieve consensus regarding where we stand or what we want to achieve. We have those for whom education is all about training for employment, and those who advocate a more liberal tradition. They rarely attempt to discuss their different perspectives and hence no common ground is found and no progress made. Hence we risk achieving neither and having an underachieving education system.

5. Education for global citizenship

'Education's purpose is to replace an empty mind with an open one.' Malcolm Forbes

This final debate is arguably the most important debate of all. Every citizen in every country recognises that the world is more global in outlook than before and that the speed with which this is occurring is intensifying. Primary education must equip children for a world which is multi-cultural and transient. Individuals themselves are increasingly likely to live in more than one country during their lifetime and even if they do not, they will meet people from many cultures and backgrounds. The current statistics suggest that around 70% of children in primary school in London were born outside of the UK, and certainly they come from a wide range of ethnic and cultural backgrounds.

The opportunity this creates for developing children with a global outlook who show tolerance and curiosity regarding those whose culture is different from their own is immense. This is the new opportunity in primary education and one which has yet to be fully embraced. An increase in global outlook does not diminish national pride or valuing of historical traditions, but it can create the citizens of the future who have a more tolerant and informed view of the world and the various people who inhabit it.

So whilst all of these themes have significance in educational policy discussions on an international level, it is this last one which has arguably the most potential for changing the outlook of children as they grow into adulthood and the possibility of increasing their aspirations to do well and engage with the exciting and accessible world at their feet.

It is also the agenda which does not need to wait for policy makers. Primary schools throughout the world are taking matters into their own hands, linking up with others in their own country and overseas and helping the children they teach become global citizens in terms of outcome and disposition.

References

1. McDonough, K. and Feinberg, W. (2003) Citizenship and education in liberal-democratic societies. Oxford: Oxford University Press

2. PISA: www.oecd.org.pisa

3. MOOCs: www.moocs.co

4. Khan Academy: www.khanacademy.org

Wider reading

Closely Observed Children: Diary of a Primary Classroom, Michael Armstrong

Learning to Teach in the Primary School, J. Arthur & T. Cremin

Able Children in Ordinary Schools, Deborah Eyre

Outliers: The story of success, Malcolm Gladwell

Pygmalion in the Classroom: Teacher Expectation and Pupils' Intellectual Development, Robert Rosenthal & Lenore Jacobson

Chapter 3

Schools are not islands

Tim Coulson

The best schools embrace being part of the unique community that is their local area and the area from which children come to the school. The best schools understand that they share the privilege of educating children with many others, but principally the children's families.

For many schools, this is not easy. Schools' neighbours and members of the community do not always see life or ways of working in exactly the same way. Teachers have the dilemma of both preparing children to succeed as members of their communities and also provide an oasis from the trials of life which all children face, and some face in abundance.

As I have the privilege of visiting so many schools across the most interesting county in the country, I am struck by the diversity of the challenges faced by schools – far more complex than the divide marked by the extent of economic disadvantage, and understood best by those who have given their entire working lives to serve specific communities. So often I hear the Head who explains to me that moving ten miles to a different school has felt like moving to a completely different cultural outlook.

Although schools are not islands, the pressures of the day to day operation of a primary school, especially a small one, pose significant challenges in how to make the time and effort to look over the turrets of the safety of the school environment. The best primary schools have always seen themselves as serving the community rather than just expecting the community to meet the school's demands and expectations.

Soon after moving to my present job, a great joy was joining a school in its celebrations with its families of the Queen's Diamond Jubilee – a celebration that will have taken place in most schools across the country. This one was special, not just because of its work on the school's history including a display of the log books (still maintained) and the great fun being had by all, but because they had the balance right that children are part of the school family and their own families.

More recently, a fiftieth anniversary of a school was marked by a garden party. As well as children performing in many different ways and lots of other entertainments, it was marked for me by hearing adults showing their children around what they remembered of their time at the school. These schools, while both with high standards of achievement and very focused on maximising pupil progress across the board, knew that to be really successful for their children, they needed to invest time and energy to contributing to, as well as expecting to receive from, their local community.

From my perspective of visiting many, many primary schools, a positive curriculum should meet the objective of both preparing children to succeed as members of their communities, and also providing an oasis which enable children to:

- attend to relationships
- articulate feelings
- develop resilience.

For those who taught before the expectations of a National Curriculum, we were both blessed and cursed by working in a much more instinctive rather than prescribed manner. Where schools plan, rather than relying on instinct, to include attending to relationships, feelings and resilience as outcomes, they will be looking to make one nod more towards recognising that there is life beyond the school gate.

Relationships

Who do you want to parent, meet or employ? A student with a first class honours degree but no 'people skills', or a student with a more ordinary level of achievement with charm, ability to make and keep friends, and an empathy for others? Do we answer the question differently as a parent or a teacher or an employer?

Curriculum is often described as knowledge, understanding and skills. There is no programme of study for relationships but we all know that some people are much better at developing and sustaining relationships than others. Successful relationships not only bring happiness and security, but the confidence to address the everyday, and occasional very serious, challenges that we all face.

School is a wonderful environment to experience great relationships. Children can observe adults who model courtesy, respect and compassion. They can develop their skills of building relationships under the expert eye of discerning adults who don't interfere in friendship building but offer a gentle prod when relationships strain and risk splintering. Crucially, the education process at its best not only enables children to learn from their experiences of relationships but to learn about relationships, what makes them work and what causes them to break down.

Effective schools are all about strong relationships, where everyone both knows what is expected, but also is given the confidence by there being a belief that they can live up to these expectations.

I have the pleasure of often being shown around schools, sometimes by Heads and sometimes by children. Both types of guide are great but you learn different information about the school. Only children tell you who are the best teachers!

As you see around the school, some impressions come over strongly, in particular the engagement levels of the children to whatever it is that the teacher has in mind for that lesson. What is very clear is the quality of relationships and the extent to which this is a factor that drives the quest for greater progress. I often leave humbled by the ambition that school leaders demonstrate to see success for particular children.

Articulating feelings

The opportunity for pupils to articulate feelings plays a strong part in many teachers' literacy lessons, as they play out the skilful blending of work across reading, speaking and writing. Some of the most engaging, and memorable, lessons touch teachers and children emotionally and spiritually as well as mentally.

The ability to articulate is one of those skills where schools have the opportunity to even up the life chances that children have by birth and parentage. Through focused and hard work, schools can help make up the gap for those not born with a silver spoon.

However, hardest of all to articulate for many are feelings, often particularly for boys. We all know the difficulties this unhelpful reserve can cause and the tragedies that can result from the lack of an outlet. Across a county with 550 schools, there are sadly always a few where tragedies are taking place, well above even the difficulties most schools know, and are the worst event in teachers' careers. We all look to ensure that we have worked as closely as possible with other agencies, but at the end of the day why people do terrible things often lies unanswered.

We have, particularly through inspection frameworks, well defined expectations of what 'Outstanding' practice looks like in achievement, behaviour and leadership. The kind of practice I have enjoyed coming across is where teachers create an atmosphere of trust and acceptance, where it is safe to experiment with the way children express their feelings and crucially can do so in a range of ways, including in art, music, writing and drama.

However, one of the simplest divides between schools appears to me the extent to which singing is given the priority it deserves within the curriculum. Many faithful teachers have sustained annual town-wide music festivals that have lasted decades (heightening how transient so many versions of the National Curriculum have been). Where singing is given sufficient priority, children have the opportunity to work together. Further, they can lose themselves in the emotion of music, and experience the articulation of feelings as composed by others, leading to subsequent expression of their own feelings.

Clear expression by children of their learning doesn't just happen but needs curriculum planning. Articulating feelings needs particular care and the fostering of a 'safe' environment in which children can feel comfortable and secure in what they say.

Developing resilience

What is it all about? Famously, the answer to the universe is 42. I spent several workshops with a wide group of people looking to agree the top priorities that would drive our work as a local authority, schools and other agencies. After much analysis, provocative contributions from invited guests, we simplified our priorities to: achieving for every child that they would be safe, happy and go to a good school. The first and third, whilst challenging, were felt to be easily understandable. The second caused much debate and led to the conclusion that were we to be able to stiffen children's resilience, the likelihood of their lives being economically and emotionally successful would be much enhanced.

One of the more geekish parts of my work is to read each week the many inspection reports generated across the county. I am constantly surprised that although many common features appear, they have remarkable differences. Some inspectors capture the heart of a school, and when the school clearly captured the inspector's heart the description can come to life. My favourite section in a recently published inspection report runs as follows:

Pupils have outstanding attitudes to learning. For their age, they demonstrate high levels of perseverance, especially when working outside. Pupils know that their efforts and ideas are valued by all staff. As a result, they are confident to voice their opinions and offer sensible suggestions about their work. Behaviour around the school is outstanding. As a result, the school is a very harmonious community. Pupils are polite and friendly to those they know and are welcoming to visitors. Dinner times are very social occasions which pupils enjoy, although many say they would like bigger dinners!

For their age, pupils develop strong values and a high level of respect for others. They have a well-developed sense of empathy. They are well aware that some of their classmates have particular needs and that they need to learn differently. They are kind and patient.

Pupils are very proud of their school and their many accomplishments, especially their artwork. Pupils of all ages have a leadership role in the school, such as class councillors or school councillors. They take these responsibilities seriously. All pupils have a strong voice in decisions relating to their learning.

I know that all of the above has been achieved through a close attention to the curriculum in this infant school and close attention to how the curriculum is not just planned and delivered, but how it is achieved.

For children and young people to thrive, it is vital that any curriculum promotes learners' resilience through:

- attention being paid in a school to developing resilience of both pupils and staff
- children taking responsibilities
- coping with not always being right, particularly for the very able child
- clear procedures, *eg* when bullying is alleged
- fostering ambition to improve on previous best.

This book is about stimulating thoughts and ideas as to how we can provide the best curriculum possible across the nation's primary schools. I welcome less prescription about how schools provide their curriculum. This in turn liberates schools to do it the way they know best for their children in their particular community. It also lays even greater responsibility on schools to devise a curriculum with rigour and challenge. The contention of this chapter is that, important as it is to address sufficiently the content of different subject areas, these are insufficient unless the same attention is paid to the vital outcomes for children which will equip them for life as active, healthy and happy citizens.

Wider reading

Book of Esther, The Bible – exploring family and ethnic relationships

Dogger, Shirley Hughes – expressing feelings about loss

The Fourth Wise Man, Fable – resilience shown by unknown member of the Christmas story

The William Tyndale Junior and Infants Schools: Report of the public inquiry conducted by Mr Robin Auld, QC into the teaching, organization and management of the William Tyndale Junior and Infants Schools, Islington, London N.1, Inner London Education Authority, July 1976 – what can happen when a school thinks it can operate without any external guidelines

The Implementation of the National Numeracy Strategy: The final report of the Numeracy Task Force, Department for Children, Schools and Families, 1998 – the introduction of a daily mathematics lesson.

Chapter 4

The values-led curriculum

Neil Hawkes

The importance of caring

In any thinking about what we teach in schools – explicitly and implicitly – the aim of education should be re-established as a moral one, that of nurturing the growth of competent, caring, loving and loveable people. Such a moral purpose encourages the development of positive character traits, thereby supporting the development of schools which are moral in purpose, policy and methods.

A negative outcome of the current education system is that too high a proportion of pupils feel uncared for in some schools. Teachers too often seem unable, perhaps through a perceived lack of time, to make connections with their students that sustain in the student a sense that adults care for them. To change this perception, teachers need to demonstrate more overtly that they care for their pupils. If pupils feel cared for, through the modelling of this quality by teachers, then they in turn learn the capacity to be more caring.

The history of liberal education is rooted in the classical education of gentlemen. It was used as a device to perpetuate a class structure by only giving sections of the community access to it. In more recent years such a liberal education is inadequate for preparing students for life. It is often not seen as relevant to them. It perpetuates a myth that the same education is appropriate for all students and does not take account of the different capacities that individuals have.

Currently, many schools focus on the logical and mathematical capacities discriminating against students who possess others such as linguistic, musical, spatial, bodily kinaesthetic, interpersonal and intrapersonal. The focus on the logical mathematical aspects with its emphasis on rationality, such as abstract reasoning, neglects important aspects associated with feelings, concrete thinking, practical activity and moral action.

Care and the curriculum

How can schools be really supportive places for children with genuine intellectual interests? The curriculum currently supports the behavioural objectives movement of teaching and then testing capacities. It ignores fundamental existential questions that motivate students.

The alternative vision challenges schools to develop the existential aspects of the curriculum, which are related to the attitudes, passions, connections, concerns and experienced responsibilities of the student. Consideration of the existential aspects of the curriculum leads to *care* being its central concept. It is not an easy option as it makes significant demands on curriculum planners, in terms of curriculum design and school and class organisation. Its aim would be to nurture the cognitive capacities or intelligences of all children.

The curriculum could feature what one writer (1) calls *centres of care*. An example would be the care of the self, which would integrate aspects such as nutrition, hygiene, physical, exercise, appearance and health. It would also look at the intellectual and spiritual aspects of the self. Topics would be arranged that would be of general concern and small groups would concentrate on specialized interest subjects. Genuine dialogue, rather than control, would be a feature of the school with the aim of shared living and responsibility. Thus, the moral purpose of education would be restored as schools become committed to the great moral purpose: to care for children so that they, too, will be prepared to care.

The traditional model of the educated person needs to be replaced with a multiplicity of models designed to accommodate the multiple capacities and interests of students. So what kind of education and curriculum should we develop if we want our children to be kind, moderate and nurturing?

Values-based education

Values-based education is founded on *the philosophy of valuing* – self, others and the environment. It implies that everything the school is and does should be based on a community agreed set of positive human values. It has grown out of the philosophical roots of education. It is based on a number of well-founded assumptions, which determine pedagogy:

- that the purpose of education is about the flourishing of humanity;
- that every child equally deserves the very best education, both at home and in formal institutions, such as schools;
- that this education should be founded on universal, positive human values (principles that guide behaviour such as respect, love, honesty and compassion), which promote an affirming relationship with self and others;
- that values need to be understood, internalised and modelled by adults; time is given for silent reflection, to promote personal responsibility and internal harmony;
- that the curriculum and lessons/activities are designed to give young people the opportunity to live the values;
- that the school's wider community is actively involved in developing and nourishing all aspects of values-based education.

When these aspects have been fully internalised, within the pedagogy of the school's community, then research demonstrates the interrelated impacts of values-based education. The research, based on the Australian Values in Action Project, (Education Services Australia, Ltd, 2010) shows five major impacts which support my assertion that a systematic and planned approach to values-based education can improve students' engagement with schooling and promote better learning outcomes, and enhance their social and emotional wellbeing. A possible blueprint for a school is set out below.

1. The whole school community (staff, pupils, parents and community representatives) is involved in shaping the values education policy.

2. A process of values identification takes place involving the school's community. A meeting/ forum is set up to facilitate this process.

3. Core positive values (*eg* respect, honesty, dignity, co-operation, peace, happiness, empathy) are identified. These are chosen through a careful process, which involves thinking about what qualities (values) the school should encourage the pupils to develop. One model has 22 values introduced over a two-year cycle – one value each month.

4. In the light of the values identified, the school decides the principles that will guide the way adults behave. Elements will be discussed to determine these such as:

    - how adults will care for themselves and each other
    - the emotional literacy of adults
    - the needs of the pupils
    - the way pupils are treated

5. Adults in the school commit themselves to work towards being role models for values education.

6. The school's institutional values (*ie* how the school is perceived by the community through aspects such as how parents are welcomed) are reviewed to ensure consistency with the values education policy.

7. The school considers how it will encourage reflective practices that will lead to values-based behaviour, such as silent sitting, active listening and the consideration of ethical dilemmas.

8. A programme is established for learning about values, which may include:

    - introducing values in a programme of assemblies;
    - one value being highlighted each month;
    - each class teacher preparing one value lesson each month;
    - the value of the month being the subject of a prominent display in the school hall and in each classroom;

- newsletters to parents, explaining what the value of the month is and how they can be developed at home.
- aspects of the curriculum (everything the school does) are identified that could make a specific contribution to values education. The range of skills, knowledge, attitudes and understanding to develop in the pupils is established. Of crucial importance is to ensure that the process of developing values education is well planned, monitored, evaluated and celebrated in order to keep the process alive and constantly under review.

The research evidence conclusively shows how values education can transform curriculum, classrooms, relationships and school environments, teacher professional practice and parents' engagement in their children's schooling. The Australian research has made a major contribution to the understanding of what good values education is and can achieve and thereby make a significant contribution to the whole purpose of schooling. The impacts can be summarised as follows:

Impact 1: Values consciousness

Deliberate and systematic values education enhances values consciousness. For instance, students, teachers and parents developed an increased consciousness about the meaning of values and the power of values education to transform learning and life. Such increased awareness was more than a superficial understanding of values but was related to a positive change in behaviour. Teachers thought more deeply about their teaching and the values that they modelled both in and outside of the classroom. Students reported on how a values consciousness had impacted on their actions, which had become more altruistic.

The establishment of communication about values between teachers, students and parents through newsletters, community forums and artistic performances, had very positive effects. For instance, giving time and space for teachers and parents to be involved in their children's values education both enhanced relationships and afforded time for parents to reflect on their own values.

Impact 2: Wellbeing

Students' wellbeing was enhanced through the application of values-focussed and student-centred pedagogies, which gave time for them to reflect deeply on the nature of values and what these mean to them and others. Such pedagogies included silent sitting, reflective writing, multimedia production, drama performances and poetry writing. In thinking about, acting on and feeling values, students developed feeling of self-worth, empathy and responsible personal behaviour. Evidence from the data showed that values education had a very positive effect on the sense of self of students who are 'at risk', marginalised or disadvantaged.

Students developed a greater understanding of the impact of their actions on the wellbeing of others. Values education helped students and teachers to look inside themselves and really work out what they value and who they are. There was compelling evidence that wellbeing impacts were experienced by teachers, parents and families, and in classroom and whole-school environments.

Impact 3: Agency

Agency is the capacity of individuals to act independently and to make choices and act on them. The evidence showed that values education strengthened student agency when it involves various forms of giving, outreach and working in the community. Agency was developed through meaningful real-life experiential learning across the curriculum, such as in the engagement in community projects, when there was opportunity for the development of student voice, initiative and leadership; and an explicit focus on ethical, intercultural and social issues.

Structured reflection on their experiences and learning was a central element in developing agency. Such activity generated a deep sense of 'self' and 'others'. For values learning to take place activities have to be deeply personal, deeply real and deeply engaging. Relationships between students and teachers were enhanced through such activities. This research finding has wide implications for teacher agency and teacher education in terms of understanding appropriate pedagogy in the context of enquiry-based curriculum.

Impact 4: Connectedness

The research showed how values education builds positive and wide-ranging connections between teachers, students and parents. It supported student engagement in learning, improved parent engagement in their children's learning and allowed teachers to develop new relationships with their students, each other and the parents and families in their school community. This was done through shared goals and practices in values education, which led to the development of mutual feelings of respect, trust and safety; and varied opportunities for collaboration within the curriculum.

The research findings show further that the values led to improved stronger relationships between teachers, students and parents, *eg* more respectful behaviours in the classroom, school and home. Community engagement led to quality outcomes for teachers, students and parents.

Impact 5: Transformation

Change and transformation was at the heart of the values projects and was the result of teachers and students being urged to engage in continuous reflection on the actions they implemented in their schools. Key changes were in changes in professional practice as well as personal attitudes, behaviours, relationships and group dynamics. Transformations were experienced and observed by teachers, students and parents alike.

The data points to profound transformations in student learning. Students developed deeper understanding of complex issues, *eg* how students can take on sophisticated concepts when they are explicitly taught and change their attitude and perception of a value. Students and parents experienced personal change and reported changes seen in others. For instance a student said how the class had positively evolved and that values had helped them to become more mature, adjusted kids. The research showed the profound professional and personal transformation that can result when the parent community is involved in students' learning.

Curriculum of the future

Around the world, countries, such as Singapore, are searching for ways to help schools to improve academic standards, positively affect student character and engage with parents and the community. Adopting the philosophy and practices of values-based education, as a whole school initiative, will, as the research shows, have a positive impact on all these elements.

Education is about the moral process of helping students to be well educated – the best people that they can be – and by so being create a more civil, educated and sustainable society. Educational philosophers have sought, usually implicitly, to address the question about how young people can be educated about values and live them in their lives.

The explicit philosophical and theoretical framework for values-based education lying at the heart of the curriculum, is in response to this moral imperative and its rationale is rooted in a long tradition, which has considered the aim of education as being a moral one. In my view, the curriculum and school of the future must be values-based in order for humanity to flourish.

References

1.   (1) Noddings, N. (1992). The Challenge to Care in Schools. Teachers College Press, Teachers College, Columbia University.

For further information contact Dr. Neil Hawkes: www.values-education.com

Wider reading

Man's Search For Meaning, Viktor Frank

From My Heart: Transforming lives through values, Neil Hawkes

The Mindful Brain, Daniel Siegel

The Storyteller, Jodi Picoult

The Demise of Guys: why boys are struggling and what can we do about it, Philip Zimbardo & Nikita Duncan

Chapter 5

Computers in learning: challenging a few orthodoxies

Chris Yapp

Visions of technology across the curriculum predate computing within the 20th century. At various stages schools' radio, cinema, TV and the video recorder have all been touted as a technology to transform teaching and learning in classrooms.

Within the computing era, teaching machines, computer assisted learning, the internet and world wide web, interactive whiteboards and virtual learning environments have all been hailed as the next big thing. Phrases such as 'Tablets will transform education as we know it' can be heard routinely from conference platforms. In the next few years such claims will be made about 3D printing, augmented reality and a host of other new technologies.

Passions are roused in the media and in schools about children becoming anti-social, locked behind computer screens and hooked into chat lines. Some schools ban mobile phones while other embrace them as a tool to empower learners. Thirty years after the Microcomputers in Schools initiative in the UK, battles between advocates and 'nay sayers' about educational technology can feel like Swift's big enders and little enders in *Gulliver's Travels*.

If we are to find a professional consensus, how do we build the evidence which the policy makers, Headteachers, teachers, parents and governors can broadly agree so that technology is used appropriately to achieve the best education for our rising generation, *and* develop teachers confident and capable of exploiting technology potential for all learners across different curriculum areas?

As adults the problem is that we focus on the new technology because of our unfamiliarity with it. If you see a six year-old child using a tablet at a speed we can't comprehend or follow, we wonder who taught them or how do they do that. If we watch that same child engrossed in a book, we can feel comfortable because we understand the experience from our own reading. Yet the truth is we can only find out if and what the child is learning by talking with them or asking questions. The appearance of reading does not mean that learning is taking place.

What we need to assert from the start is that teaching and learning are social constructs. Learning is not an industrial process that can be automated. So what we need is a framework to think about the choices we make which optimise the technologies we use for the learning and curricular outcomes we desire.

Probably the single biggest challenge over many years of IT in schools and colleges is time. I've had teachers and Heads say that they would love to embrace the technologies, but there is no time available to learn and become confident in the technologies themselves. There is no doubt some truth to that, while equally it is fair to say that some professional resistance does exist. Over the years, that same comment has been made to me in the fields of finance, retail, health and other sectors, so teachers are not alone.

The Solow Paradox

I stumbled into educational technology by what turned out to be a happy accident 25 years ago. While working for the Computer Company ICL I was involved in a multi-year research programme, 'Management in the 1990s' at the Sloan School of Management at the Massachusetts Institute of Technology (MIT). The heart of the work was addressing what was known as the Solow Paradox. The economist Robert Solow had observed, 'You can see the computer age everywhere but in the productivity statistics.'

Twenty-five years later the biggest change is that technology potential which was only in the reach of big business and governments is now in the hands of many children by the start of primary school. This enormous global industry appeared then not to produce better outcomes for organisations, be they public or private. What was it that was missing?

Let me make it plain where I stand on this issue. There is no direct link between organisational outcomes and investment in IT. The link comes in three ways:

- organisational design
- organisational processes
- people and roles.

To create sustained improvement in educational attainment using IT in schools, the challenge is for policy makers, Heads and teachers to think through these three linkages in terms of the technology potential. Let me illustrate these with a few examples, particularly thinking about curriculum planning, and deployment of staff and resources.

Organisational design

By organisational design, what I mean is a teacher in a class teaching a subject. What is taught is determined by the resources within the school and the classroom. Yet in a world of pervasive communications, does this have to be so?

If a child and their parents want to learn say, Polish, does the fact that the school doesn't have a Polish teacher make that impossible? There have been numerous examples of the use of video conferencing and other technologies to create 'virtual classrooms' so that children in different schools, sometimes in different countries, can learn together.

In one project I was involved with, we had an 'artist in non-residence'. An art teacher in a school worked with the children in class and a professional artist working in his studio connected over the internet. Another example was an astronomy club in a school working with astronomers in a university accessing a telescope in the southern hemisphere.

I am not suggesting that these should be readily replicated, scaled or made compulsory. For curriculum planners, the first challenge is to identify the educational priorities where connecting the school to the outside world using IT can help teachers and learners alike. For a small school, could access to teachers remotely help with viability and breadth of subject coverage? For a school wishing to build better links to the community, or the world of work, for instance, how can IT make these challenges more realisable?

Organisational processes

By process I wish to cover both teaching and learning, but also school administration. It is here that the focus on time can unlock the greatest potential. The best way I know to illustrate this is to look at multiple-choice questions.

A teacher has thirty pupils: if the tests are carried out on paper, the teacher has to mark them and that takes up time. By automating them, the tests can be marked by the computer freeing up teacher time for feedback, coaching and of course personal development. Another benefit is that the questions can be delivered in a random order, making copying or cheating much harder.

One example I am particularly fond of was an English Literature teacher. She gave a class of children the task of creating a set of questions about a set text. Each group of children was given a single chapter. The competitive nature of the children meant that they wanted their questions to be hard and to get the other groups' questions right. By using the computers to create a quiz show format, they were more motivated. Her experience was that they learned the facts faster and she was able to concentrate on the principles and development.

It is this type of teacher creativity combined with IT that has the potential to transform our curriculum offer, not the IT alone. I often argue that any teacher who can be replaced by a computer should be. Of course, the important thing to notice is that to enable this type of example to flourish across the whole school landscape takes time, training and confidence.

One of my favourite examples of pupil creativity was in music. I met a music teacher who wanted all the children to become interested in music by becoming composers. She explained that more of her pupils wanted to learn an instrument once they had written their first song. A music programme on a computer created that possibility.

So, the real lesson for curriculum planners is that IT in schools cannot be justified in educational attainment alone. What are the activities that go on in a school that could be done by computers to free up time to give educators the space to develop new practices? Many teachers and Heads complain of over bureaucratic forms, questionnaires and data collection overheads. How can these administrative procedures be simplified, streamlined and reduced in impact in terms of time and cost?

People and roles

The final part of the jigsaw lies in people, their skills and roles. Advances in technology in education and elsewhere render obsolete some skills and increase demands elsewhere. What happens outside education frequently is that new specialisms can be created and also a greater focus on collaboration and team working.

One example which impressed me was on a trip abroad. The school had all its homework submitted electronically. For some children who needed additional support this created an interesting opportunity. Instead of a history project being marked by the history teacher it could be sent to an English teacher and the history teacher, and marked in parallel by both. Again, notice the focus on time. Schools are busy places and finding the time to support individual learner needs can be problematic. In this case, some of the marking was done by staff outside school who were paid as assessment advisors. The English teachers had access to all the pupils' written work, not just the English syllabus. Here we can see team working and new skill sets and roles facilitated by computing supporting educational objectives.

Learning technology versus learning *technology*

So for those thinking about new opportunities within a new curriculum, don't fall for the 'Technology X will transform education' line. IT in schools *can* transform the experience of education and learning. To do that, this would be my set of goals.

1. Use IT to free up teacher time to develop their skills and practice.
2. Rethink the organisation of the school to connect the school to other schools, cultural institutions, workplaces and the local community to support the curricular priorities of the school.
3. Identify new roles and specialisms based on experience, with a focus on collaboration and team working among staff. Invest in teacher creativity.

One of the reasons that teaching can be very stressful (as well as rewarding) is that it can be very lonely. If you are the only geography teacher in a school, contact with other geography teachers for personal development and mutual interest can be very limited.

Above all, just because young people seem to be so comfortable with technology does not mean that they are comfortable *learning* with technology.

Just because teachers are less confident with technology does not mean that their professional skills are less relevant or needed.

One of the big themes in computing today is 'Big Data'. We can now store, communicate and process huge amounts of data which even a few years ago would have sounded like science fiction. Beyond the hype there is an important message for education. We have the potential to make a long wished for goal a reality, that teaching should become evidence-based and a research-led profession.

By sharing data and information across schools we have the chance to build professionally-led evidence for what works, in the way that medicine does. Much, if not all, of educational research is too small scale to impact systemically across education at all levels. To create a world-class education system, we need to think of and develop teachers as action-learning researchers and curriculum planners. Again, the focus on releasing professional time and the rethinking of roles and skills is crucial to turning the potential into reality. What is needed globally, not just in the UK, is to move from central direction of education policy to professional autonomy and evidence-based accountability.

The great futurist John Naisbitt remarked years ago: 'the more technology there is in the environment, the greater the need for the human touch'. There is nowhere this is more true than in schools. That will not be quick, or easy, but the rewards for learners and teachers alike will be more than worthwhile.

It is too easy to fall for the shiny new tools. They can be very seductive I know. Taming advances in IT to learning outcomes demands leadership and creativity from the professionals themselves. It is in the rethinking of the organisation of schools and their curriculum delivery, and the development of new evidence-based practice, that the potential of IT in education can be realised.

Let's talk about *learning* technology, not learning *technology*!

Wider reading

Future Files: A brief history of the next 50 years, Richard Watson

Civilization, Niall Ferguson

IWoz: The Autobiography of the Man Who Started the Computer Revolution, Steve Wozniak & Gina Smith

Are you smart enough to work at Google?, William Poundstone

Chapter 6

The advent of a boutique curriculum

Rob Stokoe

The purpose of education is the growth of individual potential. The function of teaching is to assist discovery, encourage creativity and to stimulate curiosity. For each of us our raison d'être is to live our own life; a life that is engaging, challenging, safe and enjoyable. As we think about a new curriculum framework, we believe that a curriculum for the 21st century must encourage the personal and intellectual growth of our young people; they are our greatest resource.

A 'one size fits all' approach will not do. A highly personalised, skills and learner focused experience for our students, *a boutique curriculum*, is required.

In articulating a vision for great learning and teaching for our international 4 – 18 school, the learning pathway is an evolving framework of outcomes designed to align pupil learning, personal development, curriculum, pedagogy, standards and assessment to support 21st century learning. Student outcomes within this boutique style approach include skills and habits of mind with a clear focus upon the unique needs of each learner, enhancing individual and collective capacity.

Inquiry based learning is question driven

The nurturing of curiosity in our students through the development of a thinking curriculum, where the search for questions far outweighs the search for answers, is core to our work. As 'curiosity instigates intellectual activity and is a central ingredient to a fulfilling life' (1), we are developing a child centered curriculum infused with inquiry. We are encouraging our students to engage actively in rich learning experiences within a learning paradigm which encourages independent and critical thinking to assist them in becoming powerful learners.

There are no limits to a child's sense of wonder and curiosity and if we are focused upon growing individual potential, we require a curriculum which allows for greater flexibility. Our teachers, as effective knowledge professionals, have the role of creating an atmosphere where students feel comfortable about raising questions and curious and enthusiastic about facing and meeting challenges. We must leave the ideas, the solutions, the questioning and the excitement where it belongs, with our students.

Less often are we now focused upon 'pure' subjects in the primary years.

Instead we engage with topics as a means of harnessing interest and promoting effective learning. *How* students learn is now given as much importance as *what* they learn. Each topic or project is treated differently, with consideration to thoughtful, connected and authentic ways to incorporate skills including critical thinking, problem solving and communication and information literacy.

Our goal is to create situations where our students love learning, seek challenges, value effort and persist in the face of difficulty. Our pedagogy and learning context seeks to develop secure, safe learners, actively engaged in a context which energises, stimulates curiosity and values open questioning. Our classroom environments are where it is 'hands up' to *ask* a question rather than to answer one.

What students need to learn, how they learn and the sustainable quality of their learning is central to our curriculum. Goals within our curriculum define successful, intentional learners, self aware individuals capable of continuously developing their capacity to learn, playing an active role in their own learning and demonstrating essential core skills in literacy and numeracy. As learners they need to be creative, productive and discerning users of a variety of technologies in all areas of learning. Key skills include the ability to think deeply and logically, to be creative and innovative and persistent in solving problems.

Students are individually focused but have the ability and skills to work collaboratively, continually sharing and communicating their ideas and their thinking. Most importantly our intentional learners see connections in their learning; this drives them to know more. Projects centred on real life learning, including entrepreneurship projects, enable learners to amalgamate a wide variety of skills and disciplines with pupil, parent and staff voice feedback demonstrating an overwhelmingly positive response to the learning opportunities created. Alongside this we are continuing to focus upon personal attributes such as honesty, resilience and respect for others, each becoming confident and capable individuals with a strong sense of self worth.

Play must continue

We need to build upon the strengths of the Foundation Stage curriculum which currently provides an outstanding initial experience of school based education, strong on skills development with a clear focus upon experiential, social and collaborative learning in both formal and informal situations.

There is a growing awareness of the need for greater coherence as we transition through Key Stages one, two and three (probably a dying terminology in our schools). Thankfully the learning potential of play has extended well beyond the foundation stage; no longer is play viewed as a distraction or 'off task' pursuit, rather a central driver for focused learning and exploration. In the words of John Dewey: 'To be playful and serious at the same time is possible, and it defines the ideal mental condition' (2)

Core skills will always need to be strong

Our students will always need to read, to write and to calculate effectively. Reading, an abstract art and one of the most complex challenges in education, is central to achievement and the growth of our learners. We are continually striving to develop a positive disposition towards reading in our students; reading as a vital tool, not just for research but for the enjoyment of discovery and engagement with imagination.

Furthermore, we are seeking to provide a context where our students listen carefully to and connect with the ideas of others, essentially encouraging the development of an empathetic learning style. This approach is actively supported by our teachers who encourage questioning, listen and facilitate the individual growth of each and every student – teachers who are as keen to learn as any child.

The delivery of this style of curriculum requires highly skilled, confident and collaborative educators, dedicated to lifelong learning and deeply committed to this whole school approach. Our diligent and innovative educators are the key drivers in supporting our young people who merit a flexible and responsive curriculum, relevant to their unique learning and developmental needs.

Interdisciplinary, project based and research driven

There is no question that the new technologies have changed the way our students learn. Technology has the potential to do many things, a new way to do old tasks or a way to make learning highly efficient and foster deeper levels of engagement and understanding. Clearly digital technologies have expanded the learning paradigm to a continuous learning experience.

In creating an agile learning environment we are integrating an array of technologies, as powerful learning tools, in a way that enriches the curriculum and enhances pedagogy, empowering learners and their learning. Ebooks provide opportunities to record, share and publish new knowledge as well as offering highly personalised feedback opportunities; pupils at our school have responded very favorably to audio feedback from teachers and their peers in their ebooks.

We are rapidly moving away from the mindset of teachers as content experts toward the concept of learning which is subject to discussion, questioning and negotiation rather than one of imposition. This enhancement of the teacher's role is enabling our students to navigate the wide array of resources available to them. Students are encouraged to seek out knowledge, to discriminate effectively, to use resources to support the acquisition of new knowledge and skills. This new knowledge, constructed through research and application, is more often being linked to real life situations and previous experiences.

With support from our educators, students skilfully organise new information, constantly refreshing and renewing their thinking, continuously growing their potential. Assessment is now focused on differentiated experiences and outcomes, with success criteria effectively scaffolding students learning.

In our own international context an evolving process of growing a learning culture that values rich discussion and focuses upon students' questions is well underway. Our belief is that the quality of discussion, the critical act of questioning and the active listening role of the teacher combine to encourage intellectual confidence and personal growth for our students.

Our students are positive, willing learners who openly accept challenge and are confident in a discovery context. The development of science discovery corners for instance, allows students in the early years, not only to dress up and act like scientists, but to explore and demonstrate their natural curiosity as they encounter new materials and experiences. Carefully selected materials inform new challenges where the questions raised during their exploration are the intended outcome of the activity. Teachers are planning for inquiry, tapping into student curiosity and the sense of wonder within each child. They are carefully developing opportunities for children to organize their learning in such a way that it supports the ongoing acquisition of skills, knowledge and attitudes at their individual level and pace of learning.

Effective educators within our school are promoting focused discussion, actively listening to students and encouraging questioning; it is really interesting to watch high quality teachers resist the temptation to talk! Teachers are intentionally modeling key learning attributes including enthusiasm, engagement, listening and sensitivity.

Great timing is key in this process; selecting the right question at the right time, offering questions that are open-ended to promote thinking and pupil led learning takes intentional practice. Learning pathways are often semi-structured, facilitating teachers in planning, thinking and responding flexibly, allowing for varying pace which supports the individual learner or group. The most interesting challenge – for teachers and Headteachers alike – encountered in the context of this boutique style education is that in some cases learning will not have a clearly defined end point.

Our own 21st century curriculum has developed as project-based, research driven and interdisciplinary, with students and educators collaborating in the pursuit of learning within and beyond the classroom. Our educators, fantastic orchestrators of learning, are enriching the lives of our students as they engage them in a curriculum which develops an integrated knowledge base, alongside promoting positive habits of mind and enabling them as happy, confident lifelong learners.

Leadership today and tomorrow: Blue Ocean thinking

As educational leaders we demonstrate our passion and dedication. We must be relentless in the pursuit of achieving excellence for our students, helping them to become better than they think they can be.

Excellence can be obtained if you:

- care more than others think is wise
- risk more than others think is safe
- dream more than others think is practical
- expect more than others think is possible.

A school is a living thing – there is no equilibrium. The rapid nature of change today and the non-linear nature of change have the potential to cause difficulty, particularly if we promote rigid planning and implementation expectations, for example in relation to the introduction of a new curriculum framework. A flexible responsive approach to both school and human development can also provide the potential and opportunity for new paradigms, new success, new dimensions in teaching and learning and creativity.

We should consider moving away from a benchmarking process against the competition as the more we benchmark against our competitors, the more we risk looking like them; we can still monitor them. Our target should be to create a future for our community as a 'Blue Ocean'.

In our 'Blue Ocean' schools we will continually challenge and progress as learning organisations, avoiding the trap of, 'this is what we do.' Staff will be able to look for opportunities which develop their skills and pedagogy beyond their current thinking and expectations. Most importantly they will have a mindset founded in lifelong learning, a commitment to self, team and school.

As leaders our challenge is to:

- create uncontested space as a centre of excellence
- make the competition irrelevant
- design new paradigms in teaching and learning through the curriculum.

As we define and develop our individual 'Blue Ocean' schools we need to be confident enough to take considered risks, to adopt an approach of slow continuous change: adapting and growing our schools, offering sustained high performance as well as increasing levels of personalisation and innovation.

It is insufficient to only have a dream or a vision. Nor is it appropriate to resist a better future because, 'this is how we do things'. On our doorstep in Dubai is an outstanding example of excellent leadership encompassing vision and execution. HRH Sheik Rashid and HRH Sheik Mohammad have turned little known Dubai into a breathtaking display of the impossible made possible. Dubai as a place is a great act of vision, drive and charismatic hands-on

53

leadership, one of pure imagination. Visionary leadership combined with excellence in execution is deepest 'Blue Ocean'.

When we challenge, really challenge ourselves, it will be our wise mistakes which create different and better futures. Our job is to encourage staff to commit to trying new ideas, bringing new learning dimensions to our students. We need to make better mistakes, and this applies to our boutique curriculum too.

Across our schools we want our staff and students to have great curriculum experiences, offering added value and striving to make a difference. At best, schools should be an emotional, vital, innovative, joyful, creative, entrepreneurial endeavour which elicit maximum human potential. Within this context every member of the school community is free to do his or her absolute best and to discover their own greatness.

References

1. Kashdan, T (2009): Curious? Discover the Missing Ingredient to a Fulfilling Life: William Morrow

2. Dewey, J. (1910): How we Think: D.C.Heath & co.

Wider reading

What's the Point of School? Rediscovering the Heart of Education, Guy Claxton

The Genius in All of Us: New Insights into Genetics, Talent, and IQ, David Shenk

The Tipping Point, Malcolm Gladwell

Blue Ocean Strategy, W. Chan Kim and Renée Mauborgne

Chapter 7

Shaping an inspiring curriculum – home and abroad

Chris Nourse

Motivate

"Education is now less about information – as the internet holds vast amounts of that – it's much more about motivation."

So said the first man to walk to both poles of the planet, unaided. Robert Swann spoke to a group of us about his Arctic and Antarctic exploits while outside the sun burned down on the Arabian Desert at approaching 50 degrees. After his spell-binding lecture I too was motivated to learn more about 2041 (1) and the treaty which protects the largest unspoilt wilderness on the planet. He had passed through the audience an electrical current of passion, enthusiasm and positive action towards his goals that for a time made anything seem possible.

Reflecting on this experience and exposure to an intrepid explorer makes me ask some of the perennial questions again: what shall we learn? Why should we learn it? How could we learn it? Where is it possible to learn it? Today our children learn online, at home, in holiday clubs, in outdoor environments, in master classes, and, yes, in classrooms.

Given Robert Swann's encouragement, how can we as school leaders take the opportunity of this new curriculum to really emphasise the GRAB factor of amazing and fascinating topics which make real demands of young learners.

Case study from Abu Dhabi

In Abu Dhabi we established a Year 2 topic to showcase the city, architecture, history and heritage of the UAE. The children were given training from a professional photographer and then shown how to edit their images digitally. The culmination of the project was an art exhibition hosted by the children in the evening with their work blown up, printed on boards and displayed every bit as carefully as a London art gallery would.

The result: wonderful learning about their city: memorable visits to the Grand Mosque, the circular building, the leaning tower, the dhows in the harbour – a deep understanding of local people and their place in time. Tangible parental engagement arose as the children served canapés and discussed the light reflecting from the mirrored office building to show the image of Sheikh

Zayed, the founder of the country. Thus, the past and the present captured in an image – by Year 2.

In my experience the more children know about their local historical context the better able they are to extrapolate this to a national and then international landscape. A compelling reason for learning about our past was given by HH Sheikh Zayed founder of the UAE: 'He who does not know his past cannot make the best of his present and future, for it is from the past that we learn.'

Gaining a sense of local identity and indeed pride has many positive spin offs. Even in areas where people perhaps feel little pride, a community project can bring people together to learn, perform, celebrate and present some cohesion to the community. We are already in a position as a world community that the fifth largest 'country' by population is made up of all those who live outside their country of birth. Sharing our values reinforces notions of citizenship even when living in another country.

In an international school with more than fifty nationalities, finding common ground to bring people together can be a challenge. In our case we decided on two projects.

Firstly, we celebrated the national day on December 2nd with a day of local culture, history, and heritage. We involved the parents in planning traditional dances, readings in Arabic and English, and the establishment of a living museum which was the focus of the day's activities. We built traditional palm houses, we ate traditional food and drink, and enjoyed the Yola dance and music.

Second, in order to include everyone's national identity we held an International Day later in the year where everyone showcased the best their country had to offer. Again we celebrated cultural similarities and differences, cultivating respect and understanding with a depth that is often hard to achieve in classroom based activities.

One final reflection on my Abu Dhabi experiences, thinking about how links *across* the curriculum can be decisive in moving forward classroom practice.

The Arabic department in the school was relatively weak and I could not speak Arabic – but I realised that effective language acquisition could be shared from one language teacher to another. So we set up some peer observations both with the French teacher and the English teachers, joint planning, focused teacher training on the three part lesson, use of high frequency words, effective use of homework, and raised the status of Arabic by offering a Masters degree course as professional development for the Arabic leader.

The impact was that the quality of teaching and learning improved, parental satisfaction improved, and the Arabic department felt more part of the school – included and integral to our wider curriculum success.

Learn from within

Schools up and down England are full of talent, yet how often do we effectively share within schools, let alone become outward facing networked learning communities? We have more to learn from each other within schools and within networks than we realize. Schools often have more inconsistencies within them than between different schools, and we need to address this as we plot our curriculum changes.

In her book *Glow: how you can radiate energy, innovation and success*, Lynda Gratton, Professor at the London Business School, discusses how important it is to get people talking within an organisation. She gives a memorable example from Unilever with whom she sorked: during a conference the *Lynx* deodorant team were sat with the Walls ice-cream team at a table. They were discussing ways to increase sales. The Walls people reported that their most popular flavour was chocolate. The *Lynx* team decided to use this information – they innovated and came up with chocolate smelling deodorant which, improbably, sold like hot cakes.

The moral of Lynda's story is that the secrets to improvement are usually already within an organisation – unlocking them is the key. What then are the most successful aspects of your school? Where does the curriculum offer really buzz? What really grabs children's interest and imagination? Is it within certain subject areas or within certain year groups? What might you do most effectively to spread the word within your own team of teachers?

Continuous change is inevitable due to the fast pace of change in the world and the political nature of the educational agenda. But more importantly than these forces are the changes in ICT which will enable improvements and innovations on a regular basis. The way we use computers in schools is clearly revolutionising education. It is my belief that tablet computers will be in regular use in all classrooms within the coming five years, with a vast range of bespoke applications to meet all levels and subject needs. The App Curriculum beckons. We need to embrace this change as part of planning, indeed as the digital natives in the Reception classes already have.

Different abilities

At the heart of a rich curriculum offer must be opportunities for all abilities, within and beyond the school day. For all pupils enrichment can be gained through visits out, visitors in, residentials, sports teams, musical activities, and master classes on anything from algebra to cooking. But what about those who need further challenge and support?

Just doing more of the same for your more able children is not enough. For your best musicians, for example, there need to be high quality master classes, access to local concerts, and trips to hear music performed by the very best musicians. Other more able students should be collaborating with other schools nationally and globally, either in person or virtually.

Debates should be happening about 'big issues' between children in Dorset and Dubai. We should be encouraging children from Andover to skype children in Abu Dhabi to discuss energy and life after the oil runs out. Children from Ipswich should be talking to children in India about their dreams and aspirations for the future. In short, technology has made it cheap and easy to contact virtually any corner of the planet – including the classroom in Antarctica. Encourage your staff to build into curriculum plans each term a different country that they contact for a specific purpose – be outward facing and excited by all the world has to offer your children.

For less able children consider different ways to engage them. Investigate Forest Schools or look at the possibility of caring for animals within school. Would your school benefit from a sensory room? Are their barriers to learning emotional ones – could you afford to appoint a counsellor? If not, could you share the costs with your local cluster? Are your teaching assistants being effectively used for curriculum enhancement? If not think again – try employing graduates and maybe more male role models for primary children.

Could you target reading for improvement and perhaps employ a reading recovery teacher to make the difference to those children? Your pupil premium funding could help here. If not, consider what you could live without in your budget to afford some of these strategies. Your spend on teaching assistants is likely to be significant; if you are not seeing the impact on the progress of the children think about why not. It may be they need further training with more specific roles. At a time of reviewing the curriculum, we need to audit and to think creatively about harnessing the skills of all our teachers and teaching assistants, so that we use their individual skills to enrich pupils' learning.

Be the centre of enlightenment for your community

For many children in the UK, the arts, music and certain cultural experiences are simply not part of their lives at home. It is often in these subjects, in those magical moments of performance or viewing great art that we feel most alive and connected to others in a shared experience. It is through these elements that children can raise their self worth and aspirations for life and learning.

Through their forthcoming curriculum development, I challenge all school leaders to shine an unquenchable light, a light to inspire many children and their families to aspire to types and levels of learning they never thought possible. Through a vision and set of values shared by the school and its local community, horizons can and should be lifted. Carpe diem!

References

1.   2041.com

Wider reading and viewing

Glow: How you can radiate energy, innovation and success, Lynda Gratton

Zen and the Art of Motorcycle Maintenance: An Inquiry into Values, Robert Pirsig

The Dead Poets Society (film, 1989)

TED Talks: www.ted.com

Chapter 8

Golden keys for curriculum leadership

Kathy Wood

Do you know a school that makes you long for childhood? Do you lead in such a school? If, as an adult you could go back to school, what sort of school would you want to go to; to learn in and to have the confidence that it was going to shape your destiny for a future that will be enormously different from what we dare to imagine?

Whatever the constraints and challenges of an individual school, is every day filled with elements of awe and wonder, high engagement with learning, surprise and laughter? Are you brave enough to be a leader of the next two generations of people, the same people who will change the future and keep what is important in our world safe and secure?

As a school leader, you need to be crystal clear on what your own 'golden keys' are to unlocking the recipe for a positive primary curriculum, fit for purpose for today and for our tomorrows.

Golden key one – how deep are you digging?

In shaping a new curriculum any leadership team should first ensure that the school has a strong sense of purpose and vision for staff, children and their families as well as the community the school serves, a vision that reflects not only the local scene but one that engages in a global setting. School leaders need to be a strong role model for their staff in thinking big and digging deep, driving forward an ambitious vision based on sound principles for learning, not waiting for and responding to the latest political driver, technique or teach-by-numbers strategy that comes in and out of fashion.

This ambitious vision needs to include a direct influence on the curriculum provision in the school. Having a clear, purposeful, well defined curriculum which meets the needs of the pupils, and one that is reviewed regularly, is critical to any school's success. Delving deep into the analysis of what exactly are the needs of our pupils is a good place to start. This needs to be aligned with the thought that our pupils are the global citizens of tomorrow who will need to overcome insurmountable challenges of say living on Mars, overcoming situations caused by world terrorism, or tackling a global disease epidemic. In turn, this will enable a leadership team to move forward with a dynamic, evolving curriculum which avoids a narrow focus and is assessed through neatly ticked boxes.

Ask yourself:

- How many leaders in your school have a leadership allowance for the development and innovation of the curriculum?
- How effective is your curriculum working party?
- How do you actually share your ambitious vision on curriculum with the whole staff and keep it alive as the years go by?

By visibly placing an importance on the answers to these initial questions, acknowledging that some may be time limited, leaders are explicitly addressing the debate, the development and the challenge of a real, fit for purpose curriculum which avoids a superficial joining-the-dots coverage. You have to make sense of the curriculum for yourself, bring it alive and make learning inspirational and exciting for both children and staff. It takes effort, conviction and passion.

Golden key two – what are your 'Values for Life?'

One response from digging deep is a 'Values for Life' approach where success is built on the ability to transform lives through 'values in action'. This values based approach powerfully reaches out to people of all cultures and faiths. It moves the spirit and touches the soul, and is a guiding light for all who want to make a qualitative difference to their own and other lives.

A 'Values School' is a 'can do' school which promotes the positive at all times. After the initial stage of implementation, the challenge for any leader is to find answers to the question of how as leaders will you really dig beneath the surface of both the implicit and explicit aspects of 'Values for Life' so that anyone who walks through your doors can feel it at work instantly. It has to permeate everything that you do. The challenge is to ensure that after initial work, your provision does not remain at a superficial level. Each school has the capacity to offer a unique, highly textured experience, so that all who come in to contact with your school would know it is having a distinctive impact on the values of the children it serves.

'Values in action' means you need to review your provision through for example, the senses, so that children and staff (and visitors) can actually feel and touch values in action; they can see it at work everywhere you walk; they can hear and smell it; the spoken word promotes it in everyday conversations and most importantly there is an emotive, spiritual response. One of the ways to re-address this focus is to place greater emphasis on the spiritual, moral, social, emotional and cultural development of children. The Ofsted inspection framework has once more placed greater emphasis on this area of development and is a useful reminder to adopt a systematic approach to the teaching of core values in our schools. As a school leader, it is also important to be constantly identifying with 'Values for Life' and what this means for you as an individual and for the staff who you lead. Trust and communication are two elements that must be addressed in a practical way from the outset and revisited regularly. Without seeking a deeper understanding of these two critical elements and how they impact the running of the school, values education becomes meaningless in overcoming the many hurdles we face in effective leadership. A creative, enquiry-led curriculum which embeds an implicit and explicit values approach to learning, and is practised by all, ensures that 'Values' permeate the learning environment.

Golden key three – are you thinking big and beyond?

A strong primary curriculum is a highly complex matrix of factors woven together and delivered by a cohesive team of talented teachers and support staff. How aware are the teachers and support staff of curriculum developments beyond the immediate school doors? Leaders need to make sure their staff have a questioning capacity so that they too can model asking big questions, rather than looking inwards and following routines unthinkingly everyday and being the drummer to someone else's beat.

What are the big questions asked by children, their parents and staff at the start of every new theme? Such healthy review and debate keeps a curriculum alive in a school. In reality, and alongside everyday pressures, staff often are not given sufficient time to engage in discussion about effective pedagogy and the lessons to be learned from regular review and sharing of knowledge. Successful, highly effective schools do this naturally, and look outwards for the benefit of their pupils and staff.

In our own context in Brunei (1), thinking 'big and beyond' goes some way to challenging the mentality that staff working in the international setting will not be as competent or as up-to-date as a teacher working in England. The recruitment strategy followed and the subsequent appointment of staff is critical to ensuring a positive primary curriculum. Together, the quality of the people in your team, and the collective high expectations they hold of what children can achieve, can determine the vibrancy of the curriculum and whether it is meeting the needs of the next generation of world shapers, doers, thinkers and leaders

Golden key four – how do you get everyone involved?

The ingredients for an inspirational, dynamic and engaging curriculum cannot be left to chance but must be prepared, mixed, and presented well. The mix will include a clearly stated purpose and vision, as well as a motivated and enthusiastic staff team who are not afraid of asking big questions. But a curriculum is nothing unless the children and their parents are highly involved from the outset. Children and parents all over the world want their children to be successful at school and to have fun. This actually means they want their child to be literate and numerate and be confident to speak up and make sense of their ever changing and complex world.

Increasingly, parents are valuing the ability to speak a second or third language and they are undoubtedly proud when their child excels in sport, music and dramatic performance. The challenge for leaders is to gather together all these aspirations and make sense of them for our children and parents. If we are doing this successfully, we ensure elements of awe and wonder, the excitement to learn, and the knowledge that the attainment and progress made is at least good, often at an excellent pace. Some questions to explore on the subject of family engagement might be:

- How do you configure an open study area? Is it sufficiently engaging for the whole family, and are opening times right?
- How much are your parents involved in their child's learning — is it fun and challenging and exciting for the adults too?
- How do you monitor and review the curriculum and involve parents in that process?
- How do you harness what parents tell you of the children's excitement expressed at home about the learning taking place in school?
- How have you developed the space and resources you have to reflect your purpose and vision around family lifelong learning?
- How do you use your community and the expertise readily available on your doorstep — and is every opportunity made to do this?

Coda: home thoughts from abroad

In any context, a school needs to be very clear in what it is setting out to achieve over set time periods. This is especially true in the international context where family mobility is relatively high, and children move in and out of international schools with some frequency.

Every child is entitled to excel and experience success in the basics of speaking and listening, reading, and writing; to be numerate and enjoy working with numbers and shapes; and know how technology can assist as a tool to access greater knowledge and understanding and develop the creative mind.

Every child should have 'awe and wonder' experiences in the arts and sports, and know how these areas can enhance the quality of their lives, developing their overall wellbeing, personal development and aspirations.

Children learn best through a rich, vibrant delivery of the basics and a balanced diet of the humanities, sciences, arts and sports delivered to a level where children and their parents feel and see outcomes which exceed their own expectations.

How you weave this all together to make sense for your pupils and their families cannot be left to chance. Creative and thoughtful leaders take seriously the job of delivering a curriculum fit for the children of today and tomorrow. They know deeply the needs of their pupils, and have a keen awareness of local, national and international trends in curriculum development. Above all, they keep focused on who the drummer is, and keep the beat strong.

References

1.   www.hornbillschool.com

Wider reading

The Primary English Encyclopedia: The Heart of the Curriculum, Margaret Mallet

Super Teaching: Over 1000 Practical Strategies, Eric Jensen

From My Heart: Transforming Lives through Values, Neil Hawkes

The Impact Code, Nigel Risner

Raising Superman, Howard L. Rodgers

Chapter 9

Which routes for your school?

Roy Blatchford

A short history

As with everything there is a history. But you have only to go back a surprisingly short way, compared say with the Napoleonic curriculum in France, to see the advent of a national curriculum in England. In 1976 Prime Minister James Callaghan, in a speech at Ruskin College, Oxford, ventured to suggest that for too long schools had operated within a 'secret garden'. He put forward, quite tentatively given the politics of the time, the notion that there might be a child's entitlement to some kind of national curriculum.

Carefully harnessing the words of R.H. Tawney – 'What a wise parent would wish for their children, so the state must wish for all its children' – Callaghan moved on to say:

The goals of our education, from nursery school through to adult education, are clear enough. They are to equip children to the best of their ability for a lively, constructive, place in society, and also to fit them to do a job of work. Not one or the other but both.

Thus began more than decade of intensive debate. Secretary of State for Education, Sir Keith Joseph, encouraged Her Majesty' Inspectorate – through a series of subject enquiries and publications – to nudge the educational establishment towards the acceptance of a nationally prescribed curriculum. The 1988 Education Reform Act finally brought a national curriculum in England into the schools' system, and the past 25 years have seen a number of revisions by different governments.

Does the curriculum matter?

Not according to many respected research studies and educational commentators. In McKinsey's influential study 'How the world's best-performing school systems come out on top' (2007) (1), the curriculum barely gets a mention. The key thrust of their report was to say that the quality of teachers and investment in their training are the key determinants of great education, alongside an unswerving commitment by those teachers that no child should be left behind. Expectations are all; the curriculum – *what* we teach – is nowhere.

Closer to home, Ofsted's report 'Twenty outstanding primary schools' (2009)

(2) placed similarly little emphasis on curriculum content as central to these schools' successes. And in my own study for CfBT (2011) (3) of good secondary schools becoming 'Outstanding', none of the Headteachers cited the curriculum as a cornerstone of how they had improved their schools. This may of course reflect the nature of how we measure our schools today, rather than Headteachers' actual attitudes to the importance of what their teachers teach.

Most intriguingly in this debate is the current coalition government's attitude to a national curriculum.

On the one hand, media coverage would have us believe that the Secretary of State would die on his sword rather than allow history to be taught in any other than the prescribed way. Speeches and articles galore have meant the content of the latest national curriculum has been served up on the front pages of our newspapers. And yet there is the following contradiction, a fissure at the heart of policy. If a school becomes an academy – and there is the political push for most to take on academy status – then the National Curriculum no longer has to be taught.

I wonder whether this 'freedom' is misplaced. Politically, it's about freeing up schools from central control. That's fine as far it goes. But look around the world. From my school inspection experiences, whether in New York or Barcelona, Abu Dhabi or Bangkok, Jeddah or Mumbai, nations retain a firm grip on their respective national curricula. They are affirming that, through a commonly shared curriculum, we are passing on to the next generation our nation's history and values, as well as preparing them for today's and tomorrow's global society.

At one level, it might be argued that the curriculum does not matter. The quality of the teacher trumps all. That said, from my own observation of more than 8000 lessons around the world over the past seven years, I think content does matter. Great lessons are rooted in richness of task; in turn those tasks are rooted in a well-planned, sequenced and imaginative curriculum which inspires curiosity, scholarship and divergent thinking amongst pupils.

What must we teach?

'The National Curriculum in England' 2013 framework document published by the Department for Education helpfully distinguishes between the *school curriculum and the National Curriculum*. For leaders and planners in schools, this distinction is a vital one. The following key paragraphs are worth careful study.

The school curriculum

2.1 Every state-funded school must offer a curriculum which is balanced and broadly based and which:

- *promotes the spiritual, moral, cultural, mental and physical development of pupils at the school and of society, and*

- *prepares pupils at the school for the opportunities, responsibilities and experiences of later life.*

   All state schools are also required to make provision for a daily act of collective worship and must teach religious education to pupils at every key stage and sex education to pupils in secondary education.

AND:

The National Curriculum in England

3.1 The National Curriculum provides pupils with an introduction to the core knowledge that they need to be educated citizens. It introduces pupils to the best that has been thought and said; and helps engender an appreciation of human creativity and achievement.

3.2 The National Curriculum is just one element in the education of every child. There is time and space in the school day and in each week, term and year to range beyond the National Curriculum specifications. The National Curriculum provides an outline of core knowledge around which teachers can develop exciting and stimulating lessons.

The paragraphs above are a powerful reminder that schools are charged with planning and teaching certain subject based prescriptions, and equally have significant freedoms to do as they choose within and beyond the school day.

Given the importance of Ofsted in schools' planning and self-evaluation, it is worth quoting from the 2012 inspection framework, with its suitably loose description of what inspectors look for:

Inspectors will consider the extent to which leaders and managers:

- *provide a broad and balanced curriculum that meets the needs of all pupils, enables all pupils to achieve their full educational potential and make progress in their learning, and promotes their good behaviour and safety and their spiritual, moral, social and cultural development*

There is certainly little prescription here; rather, a focus on educational outcomes, however schools choose to achieve them. More helpful for those leading curriculum change and development are the words to be found in the 2009 Ofsted definition of an 'Outstanding' curriculum, a definition which many, many primaries in my experience hold onto when planning and reviewing with staff and governors:

The school's curriculum provides memorable experiences and rich opportunities for high-quality learning and wider personal development and well-being. The school may be at the forefront of successful, innovative curriculum design in some areas. A curriculum with overall breadth and balance provides pupils with their full entitlement and is customised to meet the changing needs of individuals ups. There are highly tailored programmes for a wide range of pupils with different needs. Cross-curricular provision, including literacy, numeracy and ICT, is mainly outstanding and there is nothing less than good. As a result, all groups of pupils benefit from a highly coherent and relevant curriculum which promotes outstanding outcomes.

In thinking about curriculum content ahead, planners may also wish to consider the following extract from the 2012 Teachers' Standards. The Standards indicate that all teachers must demonstrate good subject and curriculum knowledge and:

- have a secure knowledge of the relevant subject(s) and curriculum areas, foster and maintain pupils' interest in the subject, and address misunderstandings

- demonstrate a critical understanding of developments in the subject and curriculum areas, and promote the value of scholarship

- demonstrate an understanding of and take responsibility for promoting high standards of literacy, articulacy and the correct use of standard English, whatever the teacher's specialist subject

- if teaching early reading, demonstrate a clear understanding of systematic synthetic phonics

- if teaching early mathematics, demonstrate a clear understanding of appropriate teaching strategies.

There are clear implications here for in-service training and for primary schools to think carefully about the relative merits and skilful deployment of subject specialists across the curriculum. Perhaps a few orthodoxies around the centrality of the generalist teacher need challenging? For example, in relation to mathematics, art and music, which teachers are best qualified to promote scholarship for Years 5 and 6?

What might we choose to teach?

From visiting hundreds of infant, junior and primary schools across the country in the past few years, my judgement is that in the vast majority there is thoughtful and creative curriculum planning (evidenced in Headteachers' and teachers' voluminous folders), allied to expert harnessing of lively and engaging resources. Few primary schools in this country want for rich resources.

In the best practice, staff have given careful consideration as to how the curriculum meets the particular needs of its own pupil population. The core skills remain an unequivocal focus throughout the school day, and the new National Curriculum is heavily weighted in content towards English and mathematics. Equally, irrespective of rural or urban context, good primary schools root their curriculum in a balance of local, national and international themes. It can surely be no other way than that, given our mobile, global society.

All schools have, by definition, their current curriculum as a starting point. As schools look ahead to shaping the new National Curriculum within their own overall curriculum vision, what models and influences might they look to in order to refresh classroom experiences and practice?

Set out below are a few possible alternatives. They are not mutually exclusive and are presented in the spirit that primary schools throughout the years have begged, borrowed and stolen ideas in order to put before children, in Matthew Arnold's words, 'the best that has been thought and said'.

One

Howard Gardner's book *Five Minds for the Future* offers this prospectus: he believes all of us in contemporary society need the following kinds of minds. Might a school forge a curriculum around these intended outcomes?

- The disciplined mind, schooled in basic subjects such as history, science and art but, crucially, a master of one profession, vocation or craft
- The synthesising mind, which can make sense of disparate pieces of information
- The creating mind, capable of asking new questions and finding imaginative answers
- The respectful mind, which shows an appreciation of different cultures
- The ethical mind, which enables one to behave responsibly as worker and citizen.

Two

The well established International Primary Curriculum (IPC) has a distinctive approach, set out in the following goals. Might your school wish to take on the IPC model in part or in full? How might your current curriculum be influenced by these goals or by some of the unit themes?

- **Subject goals**: Language Arts, Mathematics, Science, Information Technology, Design Technology, History, Geography, Music, Physical Education, Art and Society.
- **Personal goals**: enquiry, resilience, morality, communication, thoughtfulness, cooperation, respect, adaptability.
- **International goals**: understanding of one's own national culture; awareness of the independence of and the interdependence between peoples.
- **Knowledge, skills and understanding**: underpinning effective learning experiences.

IPC Unit Themes

Rulers and governments	Looking at the evidence
Sustainability	Settlements
Current affairs and the media	Astronomy
Control technology	Host country and home country
Making new materials	Location (holidays)
The oil industry	Artists' impressions of the world
Health education	An historical overview
Energy and fuels	The big geographical picture
Development	Drug education
Feelings	The physical world
Investigating rivers	Migration
Myths, legends and beliefs	Sex and relationships education
Trading	Weather and climate
How we learn	Living things and space environments
Water	The Olympics

Three

One of the National Education Trust's Advocacy Schools is Red Oaks Primary in Swindon: www.redoaks.org. Since its opening in 2007, its memorable and exciting curriculum has revolved around what it terms as 'The Big Questions'.

Staff and pupils alike decide on a question, ask themselves what they want to know in answer to that question, and construct their curriculum accordingly, with detailed planning in relation to skills and knowledge acquisition and, vitally, progression from Nursery to Year 6.

The following are among the school's recent Big Questions:

- *Are there only seven wonders in the world?*
- *Does every picture tell a story?*
- *Have we left the past behind us?*
- *What will you do when I'm gone?*
- *What lies beneath and beyond?*
- *Do you have to be a hero to make a difference?*
- *What is great in Great Britain?*
- *Is there any justice in the world?*

Four

Author and futurologist Richard Watson has published a compelling read: *Future Files: a brief history of the next 50 years.* His innovation and extinction timelines 2000 – 2050 are fascinating, predicting the advent of virtual holidays, prison countries and napcaps alongside the demise of Belgium, blindness and Google.

Further, he sets out what he sees as the five most significant and enduring drivers of change over the next 50 years. Might a new-look curriculum focus in part on these trends?

- Ageing
- Power shift eastwards
- Global connectivity
- GRIN technologies (genetics, robotics, internet and nanotechnology)
- The environment.

Five

Oceans of Innovation is a 2012 short publication from the Institute for Public Policy Research which explores the future of education around the world. In an excellently conceived section on what children should learn, it comes up with the following formula:

Well-educated = E (K + T + L)

- The K stands for knowledge
- The T stands for thinking or thought
- The L stands for leadership
- The E stands for ethics.

Could your future curriculum have its ambitions for learners similarly framed?

Six

The IB (International Baccalaureate) was established in the 1960s and now runs an all-through programme of studies and diploma, from age 5–18. Well respected around the world, its content and learner profile are worth researching.

Might your new curriculum have as its starting point the intention to produce the following kinds of learners?

- **Knowledgeable**—They explore concepts, ideas and issues that have local and global significance. In so doing, they acquire in-depth knowledge and develop understanding across a broad and balanced range of disciplines.
- **Thinkers**—They exercise initiative in applying thinking skills critically

and creatively to recognize and approach complex problems, and make reasoned, ethical decisions.

- **Communicators**—They understand and express ideas and information confidently and creatively in more than one language and in a variety of modes of communication.

- **Principled**—They act with integrity and honesty, with a strong sense of fairness, justice and respect for the dignity of the individual, groups and communities. They take responsibility for their own actions and the consequences that accompany them.

- **Open-minded**—They understand and appreciate their own cultures and personal histories, and are open to the perspectives, values and traditions of other individuals and communities.

- **Caring**—They show empathy, compassion and respect towards the needs and feelings of others. They have a personal commitment to service, and act to make a positive difference to the lives of others and to the environment.

- **Risk-takers**—They approach unfamiliar situations and uncertainty with courage and forethought, and have the independence of spirit to explore new roles, ideas and strategies. They are brave and articulate in defending their beliefs.

References

1. 'How the world's best-performing school systems come out on top', McKinsey (2007)
2. 'Twenty outstanding primary schools', Ofsted (2009)
3. 'To the next level: good schools becoming outstanding', Blatchford et al. CfBT (2011)

Wider reading

Five Minds for the Future, Howard Gardner

Future Files, Richard Watson

Oceans of Innovation, Michael Barber et al

The Diving-Bell and the Butterfly, Jean-Dominique Bauby

The Spirit Level, Richard Wilkinson & Kate Pickett

Part B

Implementing the new curriculum

Chapter 10

A 4-18 curriculum imperative

Peter Hyman

The assertions

Let me start with the assertions to hook you in. Then I will try to justify.

- Children need to talk more in the classroom.
- Children need to think more.
- Children need to be given more responsibility and trust at an earlier age.
- Children need to do real-world learning not just topic work.
- Children need to redraft and critique their work to make it beautiful.
- Children need wellbeing lessons.
- Children need to be taught by subject specialists before they reach secondary age.
- Children need to be nurtured in small schools not herded in huge ones.
- Children need to be immersed in memorable, deep experiences not superficial nuggets of nothingness.
- The cut off at age 11 is a nonsense.
- The 20th century was about rows, the 21st century is about circles.

The justification

If we want to prepare children properly to be a success in the 21st century, we need to have moral purpose and a healthy dose of innovation. Moral purpose, because all organisations that are successful are built around trust, and trust comes from having a clearly defined mission; a mission based on values not just performance indicators. We need to run our schools and our curriculum around the values and attributes which we believe matter most in the 21st century.

For me, and for School 21 that I lead, these are:

- *Grit* or wellbeing – the ability to bounce back
- *Professionalism* – to know what it takes to do something well
- *Expertise* – to gain the knowledge and ability to think in a range of disciplines
- *Eloquence* – speaking and thinking in a sophisticated way

- *Spark* – the ability to think laterally and generate new ideas
- *Craftsmanship* – the techniques for redrafting and improving work until it is beautiful.

A healthy dose of innovation is needed because there is too much that gets in the way of students fulfilling their potential. We need to start by seeing the whole journey from 4 to 18. Schools with the full age range in one place can then make more sense of how students develop from their first school days to when they leave. I was struck by what one Headteacher of a 4-18 school said to me. Between the ages of 6 and 12 is when the young mind is formed, the interests, the passions, the love of learning.

In this country, I believe we have got those years badly wrong. Years 5 and 6 are cramming for SATs in most schools, Year 7 is a settling in year where students often plateau or go backwards, and Year 8 is the fallow year in secondary schools – the valley of doom year between the excitement of 'big school' in Year 7 and choosing GCSE options in Year 9. Year 8 is where the worst teachers are hidden, and students in their crucial adolescent years are left to flail their way into adulthood. So those potentially great years of exploration are wasted. All-through schools are the way forward.

A wellbeing curriculum at the centre of school culture and ethos

Are our children well? Do they have the range of techniques to deal with setbacks, and challenging lives? In the age of broken homes, fragile children, erosion of childhood, anxiety, there is a need today to develop a wellbeing agenda that goes beyond the useful homily in assembly and instead addresses in a profound way the self-belief, resilience and confidence of every child. This requires a subtle blend of hidden curriculum and formal curriculum. The latter affords opportunities for students to find their passion, something they are good at, something that makes them believe they can be a success. The former gives them the chance to know how to live life as an empathetic part of a community, to be resilient and overcome setbacks, to learn how to be optimistic, to give to others, to see humour in situations.

Children need one to one mentoring and support. They also need classes of 30 broken down into units of 15 or fewer with an adult who gives each child the chance to speak – using circle time techniques or philosophy for children.

20th century schools (and most organisations) were designed on rows – rows of children learning by rote, rows of adults listening to lectures, rows of children lined up in assemblies, rows of children taking exams, rows of politics fanatics listening to speeches. The 21st century should be designed around circles – circles of equals, assemblies in the round, small circles to discuss and explore, larger circles for sharing and exploring. Collaboration circles for teacher training. At School 21 we believe that circles enhance wellbeing and enhance learning. We have assemblies in the round in what we call the strong circle.

An oracy curriculum

Schools are right to emphasise reading and writing. No child should leave primary school unable to read and write to a high level. It is only a very few children with severe special needs for whom it is reasonable to say that after 7 years of primary schooling it is justifiable that they cannot read. But it is time that oracy or speaking, the neglected area of literacy, is given its rightful status equal to reading and writing.

Robin Alexander's epic *Culture and Pedagogy* pointed out the discrepancy between this country and most other cultures in terms of the low status given to oracy. In the new National Curriculum there is more space devoted to swimming than speaking. Good schools and good teachers are remedying the situation but there is still no Year 6 SATs that test oracy and nor does it feature prominently in the formal part of the secondary curriculum. What Cambridge academic Neil Mercer calls exploratory talk – talk for thinking, talk to explain idea, to aid group work, to analyse a text – should be at the heart of all 21st century classrooms.

The dialogic classroom is a thinking, questioning, exploring classroom – a classroom which moves beyond the dominance of teacher talk to high level pupil dialogue. Instead of a teacher asking a question and a student giving a short answer with others listening, we need classrooms characterised by fifteen paired conversations, all using protocols that aid higher order thinking. Oracy should not just be a rich pedagogy for every lesson, but involve discrete lessons as well where the different oracy skills are systematically developed: technical skills (use of voice, register, tone); linguistic skills (use of a rich vocabulary, idiom, fluency); cognitive skills (the ability to marshal an argument, analyse, probe); and emotional skills (reading an audience, building confidence, speaking in a range of contexts and settings).

School 21 is working on a project with Cambridge University to create a diagnostic tool for identifying weaknesses in oracy and a toolkit and curriculum for ensuring all children learn how to speak in a range of settings. We have oracy running through the DNA of the school: assemblies, classroom practice, and Harkness tables (12 children debating and questioning round a table).

Surface learning versus deep learning

Too much of school life involves surface learning: small bitty work in which children have not invested much commitment. Too often there are questioning techniques from teachers which involve mono-syllabic responses. There is precious little time for student reflection and for students to craft their work until they are really proud of it.

For a curriculum to work we need to let things breathe, do fewer things but do them really well. More than that we need to immerse students in rich learning experiences, and experience texts (in the widest sense) that elicit emotional connection, and therefore deeper understanding.

At School 21 we do a lot of our learning through texts. This year, for example, we studied *Wonder* by Palacio, about a boy trying to cope with school despite a facial disfigurement, as a way of discussing and thinking deeply about issues to do with friendship and bullying. More traditional assemblies on the subject would have made far less impact.

A project based curriculum

There is in my view an important distinction between topic-based learning and project based learning. Of course, it is not an either/or – both have their place – but, I believe that in the 21st century a project based curriculum will bear more fruit. The distinction is this: a creative topic-based curriculum that many schools have developed involves a theme or topic: space, chocolate, rain forests, super heroes. Some of them are brilliantly creative and involve great art work, performances, displays, poems, the integration of geography, history and science and provide real enjoyment for children. Often they are exciting but lack real challenge, enquiry or a meaningful end product that has real value.

Project based learning is different. It starts with an enquiry and ends with a real world product and a real audience. Projects often aim to make a difference. They help build community, solve a problem, and add to the history and culture of a local area.

For example, a project in which children look at disease patterns for diabetes in the local area and then present findings to the local health authority is work of value to a real audience. A project in which World War Two soldiers are interviewed and then the interviews are edited and collected in a book that is sold in the local bookshop is again a project with a real purpose. Ron Berger's *Ethic of Excellence* is the most convincing book on the merits of project-based learning. He is a primary teacher from America who believes, in his telling phrase, that school is about creating beautiful work that makes a difference and you do so by craftsmanship.

Start specialisms earlier

A 4 to 18 school provides the perfect opportunity for children to be taught by subject specialists earlier. Learning a language at four is easier than it is at age eleven. High quality science and maths from age seven or eight allow children to be inspired at the right time. Specialist drama, PE, and art teaching can unlock passions.

As Howard Gardner says in his book *Five Minds for the Future*, one of our tasks is to teach children 'ways of thinking' – how to think like a scientist or a philosopher or a historian. By nine or ten children are ready to engage in these methodologies and ready to develop their toolkit of thinking skills.

Children as leaders

At what age should pupils manage their own school improvement budget, critique schemes of work, teach other students in lessons, run after-school clubs, interview candidates for jobs, observe teachers? All these things happen in some secondary schools. Why not in primary too? We need to put children centre stage, give them a stake in their school beyond the school council.

In my recent experience something extraordinary happens in a new school that only begins with one year group. All the creative ideas that teachers have are thrown at the only children you have in front of you – in our case Reception children. The result: Reception class are doing things you never thought possible. With all year groups in a school we are too rigid in deciding that 'this is Reception work, this is Year 1 work, this is Year 2', and so on.

With those barriers removed we soon realise that Reception children can be doing Year 1 and 2 'work' quite happily, and this is a cautionary note when we look at any document such as the new National Curriculum which sets out knowledge and skills in an age-related way.

A new role for teachers, a new role for collaboration

So if we want the 21st century curriculum to be rich in English Language and oracy, have wellbeing centre stage, be designed around real world projects and be integrated into a 4-18 journey, then we will need a different kind of teacher. The 21st century teachers will have to be even more multi-skilled and collaborate in new ways. They will have to be project designers as well as phonics teachers, wellbeing coaches as well as assembly teacher, oracy pedagogue as well as mentor. This is the great challenge for the future.

Wider reading

An Ethic of Excellence, Ron Berger

Mindset, Carol Dweck

Five Minds for the Future, Howard Gardner

The Bottom Billion, Paul Collier

Websites

www.edutopia.org

Chapter 11

Aspiring to a child-centred curriculum

Will Power

'The greatest misconception that teachers have is that they assume that children come to school to learn. They don't...'

I find this view – one put to me on a recent training course – rather pessimistic. It also generalises the views of young people. But it does beg the question: Is there a fundamental disjuncture between what we as teachers expect of children and what they themselves expect of school? Indeed, there is a great discourse on the role of 'child-centred learning' and 'meeting the needs of all learners' in education. So to what extent will the new National Curriculum really reflect the needs of this nation's young people, and how far should it be driven by children themselves?

As is frequently evident in the media, the curriculum is the public battleground on which many competing versions of education are contested. This is because the curriculum *is* our vision for education: it defines what is taught and (since 1997 at least) how it is taught. It also describes the relationship between the medium of learning – the teacher – and the learners themselves. The curriculum is also an expression of our public values and, less desirable, political imperatives.

But any curriculum should work to bring the many stakeholders in education closer together. If it can narrow the gap between the expectations of those who work in education and those for whom the curriculum is designed, then the education system is much more likely to produce young people who are engaged, curious and creative – in other words, ready for the challenges of a global world. Moreover, it is this alignment of competing visions that perhaps comes closest to defining what is meant by a 'child-centred curriculum': one that is driven by children's own curiosities and informed by their own experiences of the immediate and wider world.

What is a 'child-centred curriculum'?

'Child-centred learning' is tried and tested educational jargon (some might say cliché): ubiquitous in research papers and school vision statements alike. But does anybody really know what it means? Perhaps the nature of the concept is that it relates to a multitude of experiences and so evades simple definition. Maybe it is an easier concept to experience – to see, hear and feel – than it is to reduce to a simple one sentence statement. It could be a phrase used to describe a set of tendencies, or an expression of a school's culture, rather than a prescriptive tick-box list.

The following paragraphs are attempts at concretely describing five distinct characteristics of child-centred learning based on my own experiences of good practice. These in turn could be used to inform the basis of a child-centred curriculum where learning is:

- A dialogue between teacher and learner
- Driven by children's curiosity
- Enquiry-based learning
- Relevant and meaningful to children
- Practical preparation for future life.

'If you don't underestimate me, I won't underestimate you.' **Bob Dylan**

A child-centred curriculum must accept that teachers and pupils are partners in education. It is not simply the case that pupils are 'empty vessels' or naive recipients of knowledge imparted to them by the teacher. Indeed, the democratisation of knowledge through the internet and other digital media has shown that learning can take place via unconventional sources. The fact that many teenagers (and in fact many of my Year 6 pupils) have a much more advanced grasp of open-source technologies and social networking than their teachers is just one example of how the traditional roles of 'teacher' and 'taught' have been thoroughly overtaken by advances in technology.

I would contend that examples such as these show what has long been known about the nature of learning, that it is the sum of our shared experiences: challenged, tested and reformulated to make them relevant and applicable to our own lives. A child-centred curriculum should reflect this understanding and offer powerful opportunities for children to explore the ways that they learn, reflect on mistakes, and make honest assessments of their own learning styles.

Recognising that learning is a shared experience also raises expectations of both the learner and teacher. As Bob Dylan pinpoints above, accepting that learners have a rich array of past experiences and insights to bring to bear is a key part of laying the foundations on which to build new learning which is challenging and relevant to the learner. This trust and reciprocity can be fostered through dialogue about the learning process, meta-questioning and frequent, open-ended activities that function as opportunities to elicit prior knowledge and misconceptions.

Letting children direct their own learning

It may seem self-evident that curiosity is an essential part of the learning process; to want to find out about the world is a prerequisite to actually doing so. Why, for instance would you engage in a lesson on micro-organisms if you did not care what they were or why they are relevant to our lives? Most teachers would agree that fostering curiosity is an important aspect of effective teaching. Yet, through a culture of teaching to rigid success criteria, prescriptive curriculum coverage and a fear of letting children fail, I believe that collectively we have been guilty of stifling curiosity. Setting children closed tasks may make them easily measurable for APP grids and the like, but by their very nature limit natural learning impulses.

'Child-centred' should mean 'child-led'. Again, this is something easy to say but harder to put into practice in a meaningful way. Many teachers I know would shy away from attempting child-led activities – perhaps this says something about the way teachers are trained, or more likely, the pressure they are put under to deliver clear, measurable 'data'. Nonetheless, when learning is designed to be child-led it has been proven to increase engagement and raise attainment.

Moreover, child-led activities are more inclusive because they allow learners of different abilities and learning styles to engage with a topic in their own way. In these situations it is the job of the teacher to create meaningful opportunities to scaffold children's excitement and interest in such a way that naturally moves them forward. This conforms to the maxim 'teach less, learn more', because the onus is on students to direct their own learning in response to rich, well-planned, open-ended activities.

Learning through enquiry

The best examples of this are to be found in science teaching, a subject highly conducive to open questioning and exploratory, investigative activities. Here, little more than a simple 'hook' – a stimulus to spark interest and generate questions is enough to provoke an enquiry that can last several lessons. Great examples that I have seen include bowls of rotting fruit left out on tables for children to inspect; a simple circuit that won't work; strange looking fossils. Giving children simple, clear and focused instructions to go out into the school garden and 'see what they find' can be enough to begin a discussion on organisms and biodiversity.

There is no reason why this 'investigative approach' could not apply to other subjects – maths, geography, history even SPAG (spelling, punctuation and grammar). Underpinning this is an ability to scaffold children through effective questioning and being able to provide opportunities for learning which engage all learners in a way that challenges and excites them.

But most importantly, enquiry-based learning must accept that sometimes children will get things wrong, not get answers they were expecting or lead them to dead ends. These are all valuable learning points that must be embraced because they reflect the reality of learning in a world that is as full of failures and challenges as it is successes.

Indeed, why shouldn't a new curriculum have a section for 'learning how to fail'? If it did, then perhaps we would produce young people more resilient and wise to the realities of adult life than is currently the case.

Learning in context

If learning is a process of constructing and re-configuring the world around us, then it is natural that a child-led curriculum will be an expression of a child's individual context – where they live, who they live with, their identity, their time and personal history. Does this mean that by advocating a child-led curriculum we are actually proposing an infinite number of individual curricula? Teachers and children should have the flexibility to adjust what they teach and learn so that it is meaningful to the personal context of the learners themselves.

This is not to say that topics should only include subjects that link to a learner's limited experiences. They should also include opportunities to explore shared experiences that bridge culture, gender and ethnicities, and encourage children to makes links between themselves and individuals in other times and places. Education is about broadening horizons.

Context should also include the physical environment for learning. When I asked my Year 6 pupils to draw what they thought good learning looked like, every single one drew a picture of themselves in a classroom. But learning isn't something that is restricted to the classroom, even though my class, sadly, saw it that way.

To learn is to be engaged in the world, to be curious and to be asking questions. In order to communicate this effectively then we should create a curriculum which breaks assumptions about where and how we learn and impels teachers to take their learning out into the world: into the school garden, onto the streets where children live – wherever they can to make what they teach real and relevant. It is this physical immediacy that even the most sparkling classrooms may struggle to compete with.

Learning for an uncertain future

My final point about child-centred learning and creating a child-centred curriculum relates to the purpose of learning. We have a responsibility to create a curriculum that prepares our young people for an uncertain future and gives them the best chance to be successful in their lives. We need also to give children choices so that they are free to pursue their interests in whatever way they choose. The point of a curriculum is not therefore about creating idealised citizens: young people who are mirror images of our own beliefs and values. It is about equipping our pupils to be able to adapt to a changing world, to new technologies and about them being able to embrace the unexpected, even if it challenges established orthodoxies.

Hoping for a curriculum that is 'child-led' is much more than hollow cliché; more than just a nod to where I think we, instinctively, know that learning should be – in the hands of the learners themselves, led by children and informed by their own experiences and curiosities. We must ensure that it is a curriculum that fosters curiosity, has open-ended inquiry at its heart, embraces failure as part of learning, and is relevant to the learner in the context of a truly global world.

The inevitable irony is that the reality lies too often in a curriculum created, tested and implemented by individuals who will only have distant memories of what it feels like to be at school.

We must have a commitment therefore to listening to young people and embracing learning as collaboration. Having such high expectations is how we will bridge the gap between what we expect of our learners and what they expect of us; how we will excite children to become more independent in their learning and embrace education as a vital part of preparing them for the future.

Wider reading

The Cambridge Primary Review, Cambridge University Press

Inside the Black Box: Raising standards through classroom assessment, Paul Black and Dylan Wiliam

The Society of Mind, Marvin Minsky

The Element: How finding your passion changes everything, Ken Robinson

Chapter 12

Developing independent learners

Kate Atkins

Schools in the UK have a significant challenge to face. The education system was designed for the needs of the industrial revolution when society needed to educate many people to a relatively low level of attainment in order that they could take up the new employment created in factories and industries.

Whilst many other countries in the world have modified and adapted their education systems to meet the changing global economic and social needs, the UK has clung to the model of 'chalk and talk' education, convinced of the need to impart knowledge and facts rather than seeking to create independent learners who are self motivated and filled with a love of learning. Schools have become reliant on a prescribed curriculum which tries to standardise learning rather than encourage creativity.

So far this system is not working too well. Although all statistics need to be looked at in context, what scores such as to be found in the PISA ranking tell us are that students in the UK do not do well compared with their international neighbours and, most worryingly, the education system is not equitable. This is supported by the continued discussions in the media about how to close the achievement gap. There is a significant percentage of the population that is not learning and the system still is not helping them.

Pasi Sahlberg in his book *Finnish Lessons: What the world can learn from educational change in Finland* states that the top four educational systems in the world have four features in common:

- There is no private education system
- There is no over prescribed curriculum nor standardised testing of it
- There is no punitive accountability of schools
- There is no fast track teacher preparation

Schools have no direct control over three of these features but they can control the second feature: that of a flexible, responsive curriculum. Schools can give children the opportunity to explore their own interests and passions at school. They can give them an understanding of what it means to learn and how to learn. They can give staff the chance to use their passion and the local resources to introduce new subjects and new ideas. And they can give children the chance to influence *how* and *when* they learn.

Give children the opportunity to explore their own interests

Schools should involve children in the creation of the curriculum that they will learn. There are many ways that schools can facilitate this and thus create a negotiated curriculum.

Many schools now teach subjects through a project or topic approach to learning. Many of these projects will have some kind of final output, which should highlight and evidence the learning that has taken place and gives a real sense of purpose to the learners. This sense of purpose and ownership of learning is increased by co-creating the curriculum with children at the beginning of the project. Give children the project title and some kind of provocation, and let their ideas roll.

In one Year 4 project entitled 'Our Sea – Portal, Protector, Provider' children came up with the following list of things they would like to learn about: deep sea creatures; how the moon controls waves/tides; ocean currents and whirlpools; how are beaches made; the history of the British navy; seafood, the effects of pollution on the ocean; protecting animals, *eg.* from fishing; how do you breathe underwater; marine plants; the Bermuda Triangle; Henry VIII's ships; Lord Nelson; how reefs are made.

The staff then introduced the children to the 'non-negotiable' aspects of learning, describing them as 'the things the government says you have to learn', which were: to explain why places are like they are; to recognise some physical processes and how these can cause changes in the environment; to ask geographical questions, collect and record evidence, analyse this and draw conclusions; place events, people and changes into correct periods of time; to learn about significant people, events and places in the past; to find out about the past from a range of sources; to communicate knowledge and understanding of history in a variety of ways.

There was then a discussion about how easy it would be to put those two elements together. The children could learn about a 'significant person and event from the past' by studying Lord Nelson and the Battle of Trafalgar. They could learn about how 'physical processes cause changes in the environment' by studying coastal erosion. In fact, the children were able to work alongside their teachers to plan all of their initial learning.

This approach can be extended to all areas of the curriculum. Once taught the skills they need for writing, children can apply them in a context that interests them. If children have been taught how to punctuate direct speech, it doesn't matter whether they evidence their learning by writing a story, a football match report, or a newspaper article. What matters is that they write for purpose and with interest.

Give children an understanding of how to learn

Every piece of learning that children do should be put into context for them.

They should know and be able to articulate why they are learning something, how they are learning it, and how they will know if they have learnt it. Children are much more likely to learn their times-tables off by heart when told that it is a great skill to be able to have instant recall of these facts. They should also be given a range of strategies to help them, such as quizzes, songs and computer programmes. If learning something is important, schools should make time for the learning of these skills in the classroom.

Children also need to be able to recognise *when* they are learning, and schools should teach this explicitly. Many children are afraid to make mistakes or only experience lessons where they get everything right. Schools need to develop a culture that celebrates failure as the precursor to learning. It is only when children struggle to learn something that they can gain insight into the strategies there are for learning, and how and when to use them (metacognition).

Children in primary schools are able to recognise different ways in which they learn. This is a list generated by Year 3 children when planning their project 'What's On The Inside?'

- Look on a computer
- Look in a book
- Cut it open - go inside it
- Visit a museum
- Visit it/explore
- Investigate
- Ask an expert
- Do an experiment
- Watch a video

The next step is to enable them to select a strategy independently. In one classroom discussion, Year 6 children were analysing their learning during a 'Heart Start' project. One of the boys reflected that he would like to have access to a video because it really helped him to see what should be done during CPR and because he knew that, with time, he was likely to forget and would like to be able to refer back to the video to remind him. With the help of his teacher he was able to think about how this strategy could be applied to other areas of learning, and found a website with videos of how to do maths calculations which he knew he would be able to use in secondary school to help support his learning.

Give staff the chance to use their passion and the local resources to introduce new subjects and ideas

Some children will have access to a wide range of experiences and will go with their parents, carers and families to museums, the theatre, the cinema, walking, swimming, *etc.* These children will be given the opportunity to experience many curriculum areas dependent on the interest and enthusiasms of their families. However, some children will not have these opportunities. This is where schools play a vital role in giving all children access to new experiences.

There is a real tension between standardisation and creativity. Schools must guard against a 'lottery' education system and ensure that there is equal access to educational experiences. They must also ensure that effective teaching and learning is happening in all classrooms. However, there must be the freedom for teachers to be creative and to share their passions and enthusiasms with the children.

Without wishing to fall into the either/or trap, do we really feel that it is vital that all children in Key Stage 2 learn about 'Britain's settlement by Anglo-Saxons and Scots'? Wouldn't we rather allow teachers to be able to teach a period of history which interests them, and therefore enthuse the children about history and the lessons we can learn from it? We all know from experience that a subject taught with passion is a subject taught well.

Teachers should also be given the opportunity to share expertise. In the Year 4 project about the ocean (mentioned above), each teacher picked a 'specialist subject' to teach to all the classes in the year group. Each having done their in-depth researches, one taught about coastal erosion and tides, one taught about the effect of humans on the ocean through over fishing and pollution, and one taught about Lord Nelson and the Battle of Trafalgar.

Schools must also make use of the resources they have around them to get children to understand that learning happens everywhere. From a simple trip to the park to name trees for a guidebook they are writing, to a sleepover at the Natural History Museum. There is a world of experience to be had out there. And broader, often outdoor and hands-on experiences make a huge difference to children's attitudes to learning. They widen children's interests and increase their ability to learn independently.

Give children the chance to influence how and when they learn

As well as having control of the curriculum, children should also be given control of their timetable. This can happen at a whole class and individual level. Teachers can have meaningful discussions with quite young children about what happens when in the weekly timetable, and why some things are 'non-negotiable'. Children may ask, 'Why do we have to do PE on Tuesday morning?' and the ensuing discussion gives them a sense of the difficulties involved in sharing resources (a sports hall) amongst a large community of 20+ classes.

Discussions about why there is a daily maths whole-class input from the teacher help focus on what happens when you do something every day – you remember it and you improve it. Hence the reason that David Beckham practised free kicks every day for thirty minutes, what Matthew Syed in *Bounce* (1) refers to as 'the 10,000 hours of purposeful practice'.

However, children can influence *when* in the day that input happens. They may elect, for example, to do maths in the morning when they are more alert rather than straight after lunch when their energy levels are lower. The whole class timetable should be negotiated weekly to respond to changes to the season (is learning affected by temperature?) and the school calendar.

Some schools use independent personalised tasks to practise taught skills, rather than differentiating activities straight after a skill has been taught. Learning this way also gives the children the opportunity to select when they will undertake each task. Getting them to plan and track when they do these tasks allows them to take more control of their learning. Children can work with a friend, they can complete difficult tasks first, or they can 'put off' their least favourite activity until the end of the week. Allowing these learning behaviours to manifest in the classroom gives teachers the opportunity to both challenge and support them, thereby helping children to develop secure independent learning behaviours for the future.

Listen to the learners

In 1997, Margaret Madden and Joan Ruddock wrote an article for the *Times Educational Supplement* called 'Listen to the Learners'. In it they said:

"if we are concerned with pupils' achievement we should take our agenda for school improvement, in part at least, from their accounts of their own learning.... Young people are observant and often capable of analytic and constructive comment. They usually respond well to the responsibility, when it is seriously entrusted to them, of helping to identify aspects of schooling that enhance or get in the way of their learning."

Our children have lots to say about learning, when asked. Let's ask them!

References

1.   Matthew Syed (2010) Fourth Estate. 'Bounce'

Wider reading

Finnish lessons. What can the world learn from educational change in Finland?, Passi Sahlberg

The Six Secrets of Change: What the best leaders do to help their organizations survive and thrive, Michael Fullan

Negotiating the Curriculum, Garth Boomer et al

The Checklist Manifesto: How to get things right, Atul Gawanda

Drive: The surprising truth about what motivates us, Daniel Pink

Chapter 13

For the love of learning

Katy Peters

It's boring!

As each year passes in schools it seems that the on-trend word for 'excellent' seems to change. So much so that apparently in 2013 it is quite acceptable to label something one likes as 'sick'. The lingo used by children adapts so much that as a maturing professional it is often quite difficult to keep up with the newly revived definitions for common words in the English dictionary. Surprisingly though, one word which has been used consistently throughout the years by pupils to describe their lessons is the term 'boring'.

Whilst a fairly unimaginative word, if someone commented on your hairstyle or fashion sense, rendering them 'boring', would you not seek to book an appointment at the hairdresser's or call a trusted friend to come clothes shopping as a matter of some urgency, with the intention of rectifying this judgement of yourself as quickly as possible? Of course you would – it is human nature to want to be accepted and appreciated by others.

Why is it that the term 'boring', so commonly bandied about by children in relation to school, lessons and teachers/teaching styles, has not only become an acceptable descriptor of performance within the profession but one that too few teachers seek to rectify? During training, student teachers are encouraged to reflect upon their practice and evaluate their performance on a regular basis, looking for ways to develop and improve their teaching to best meet the needs of the pupils. For those teachers recognised as outstanding practitioners, this is an exercise which they intuitively perform daily, as inherent to their success as a class teacher is the ability to not only listen but also respond to pupils' feedback, so that they continually shape the curriculum and their performance for their clients.

What is it which disengages so many of our pupils? Is it the content, the delivery or the generic approach towards teaching the curriculum to which we have become accustomed? The introduction of various initiatives over the years, such as the Literacy and Numeracy hours, whilst with good intentions of raising basic skills, have unfortunately slowed learning, failed to captivate children's interest and have rendered school tedious to many pupils. The routine safety of a scheduled lesson – spent on a ten minute introduction, fifteen minute input, thirty minute independent/group activity and concluding in a five minute plenary – has resulted in staff playing things safe, neglecting the opportunity to take risks, and promote divergent thinking, curiosity and scholarship.

Awe and wonder

The phrase 'awe and wonder' is used quite frequently in educational debate, but what does it really mean? It is just a change from this Literacy Hour four-part lesson? Perhaps it means the involvement of some new resources during the course of an activity, or it is taking the pupils into a different world (real or imagined) where they are wholly captivated, able freely to ask questions, make mistakes without fear of reprimand, and assume responsibility for their own learning?

There is no single answer, no perfect solution, but surely 'awe and wonder', in whatever form, stems from building positive relationships with your children, knowing them well and respecting them enough that you are able to listen and respond to their learning needs on a daily basis, ultimately inspiring them with a thirst for knowledge. For a moment, think back to a favourite teacher, the person who inspired you to succeed and who excited you about learning each and every day. Just Revisit that memory and consider what that professional afforded you as a child, which enabled you to learn and achieve your potential. That magic they conjured up was so powerful that it still remains with you to this day.

Equally, as a teacher you will be able to pinpoint a child in your career whose attendance was erratic, yet they always managed to appear at school on the day of the school trip. Why? Well, quite simply, because it was exciting and didn't feel like 'work'. There is of course no reason as to why that child shouldn't appear in school every day if the forecast for learning was as enticing as the trip to the seaside!

If at the heart of an exciting curriculum there is the understanding that taking risks and making mistakes are expected, accepted and valued, then children (especially the more vulnerable) are less likely to experience challenges and frustrations in their learning and will adopt increasingly positive attitudes towards both it and you. A change from passive compliance or (at worst) low-level disruption to a bubble of excitement, discussion and exploration is the pattern that teachers and leaders need to secure across all classrooms.

A simple glance into the world of learning in countries such as Norway and Sweden, where creativity thrives in learning outside, very quickly identifies the potential weakness in our own education system. The Swedish organisation Friluftsframjandet (Promotion of Outdoor Life) recognises that 'Nature is an endless laboratory, a cosy room, a room for play, a place for construction, a gymnasium and many other things.'

The inspiration for learning and the answers to all questions are held in the world around us, so why are we reluctant to escape the four walls of the traditional classroom and explore the biggest classroom of all? Is it because we feel that there are restrictions imposed by the curriculum, the school, the Headteacher? Quite possibly, we impose the restriction ourselves as we have our safe way of teaching, which ensures that we have ticked the boxes for content coverage whilst maintaining control of our pupils. However, in the process we seem to have forgotten not only the real fun that learning affords us but also the opportunities it provides for everyone, including adults, to take risks and learn in real contexts.

Early Years versus *all* the years

Much research has been conducted into Early Years' education and what children at this early stage of development require to learn in the most effective way. We openly encourage children to be creative, play in imaginary worlds, write in sand, dig in the garden and learn, with a great deal of independence and ownership of the activities available to them. Yet the minute they reach the tender age of five, somehow this pedagogy is abandoned and more formal expectations, such as recording in exercise books, sitting still for long periods of time, and learning indoors from a whiteboard and textbooks are imposed.

Without question, the Early Years' approach to education is hugely valuable and introduces children to the concept of learning in imaginative and engaging ways, nurturing learning as a skill for life, not just for the classroom. We are too quick to dismiss it, certainly in the upper primary years. Wouldn't we all rather attend a training course which is active, well-paced and allows us the opportunity to engage in the learning at a level suitable to our needs? Why then do we not afford all of our pupils the same opportunity, regardless of their age and academic ability?

No-one is denying that many essential aspects of the curriculum can lack inspiration for pupils (and quite often staff), but they are nonetheless essential skills for the future of our nation. The skill of a true teacher is to create magic when conveying the laws of science, the rules of mathematics and the techniques of art without necessarily delivering a routine four-part lesson with children sitting in ability groups of six and imparting knowledge from the front of the classroom. Of course there is a place for formal teaching methods, and these need to be put across in ways which do not lead to the disengagement which we see later in too many of our secondary aged students, who seem to have neither passion nor hunger for learning. Paul Marshall's book *The Tail* is both a depressing account of the long tail of under-achievement in the UK, *and* a powerful reminder that some schools enable some youngsters to buck the trend though high expectations and a suitably designed rich curriculum.

As professionals we need to consider how to deliver a sound education to pupils which affords them the requisite skills for the future, but perhaps challenges the traditions of the British education system and allows teachers greater freedoms to adopt the strategies and ethos which lie at the heart of learning and which have been so successfully harnessed by the likes of Singapore and Finland.

In an evolving world of technology, targets and testing, children are expected to grow up too quickly without high quality opportunities to engage in role play, talking and spending time exploring the world. From entering school at the age of three, children should be presented with experiences which nurture their child-like qualities whilst challenging them as individuals. If loving learning is to be a life-long skill for children then this manner of teaching and ethos towards primary education should be evident throughout a school not just isolated to the youngest pupils in our care.

Teaching or learning?

Teaching as a profession comes under fire all too often as an easy job with short working days and long holidays. Once upon a time a teacher was a highly respected professional and now it seems that the public perception of this role is that it can be performed by anyone. Making learning exciting, captivating and a positive experience for all pupils is by no means a simple task and its power should never be underestimated.

However, it is all too common to see teachers working harder than the pupils as they attempt to teach the children. The focus in our curriculum planning and delivery needs to shift from the teacher to the pupil. Some Headteachers are now adopting the title 'Head Learner', which highlights this concept of learning at the centre of education. It is not the duty of the teacher simply to impart knowledge to little minds with the help of a whiteboard and exercise books. It is the teacher's own love of learning which should be used to facilitate the learning of others: presenting pupils with the most appropriate and engaging of activities with the intention of achieving a specific outcome.

Adopting a more creative approach to learning requires greater effort in the first instance whilst the teacher gets used to thinking in a different way and retraining her/his mind to focus on learning rather than teaching, and on the value of each activity (and its intended outcomes) presented to pupils rather than just keeping them busy. Very quickly though, the balance changes so that the children start to learn independently and the teacher's role becomes one of an enabler, empowering pupils to determine their own methods and lead their education, with skilled teacher intervention at the most pertinent of moments to offer the next challenge or provide reassurance.

With impending changes to the curriculum and greater freedoms for schools perhaps the time has come to challenge many of the traditions associated with primary education to ensure that the quality of our education system evolves in line with other more successful countries. An approach towards curriculum delivery which captivates all learners, engages each of the senses, promotes independence and affirms success on a daily basis is surely the solution to positive learning behaviours, successful individuals and ultimately 'Outstanding' schools.

The French author Victor Hugo once observed: 'He who opens a school door closes a prison.' Without question, a highly literate and numerate person is more likely to be successful and will forge out a career path for him or herself. However, upon opening a school door to provide children with key academic skills we are also responsible for growing them as confident human beings who are abundant in self-esteem, willing to accept challenges, grounded in morals and manners, and who have been exposed to the love of learning as a life-long skill which they will value forever.

Wider reading

The Outdoor Classroom: a place to learn, Harriet Harriman

Learning Outside the Classroom: Theory and Guidelines for Practice, Simon Beames, Pete Higgins, Robbie Nicol

The Tail, Paul Marshall

Teacher Man, Frank McCourt

Classroom Creatures, Gervase Phin

Chapter 14

A tapestry curriculum

Dave Smith

In announcing the revised National Curriculum in the summer of 2013, the fanfare headline on the gov.uk website read '*Education reform: a world-class curriculum to drive up standards and fuel aspiration*'.

Courageous words, but on reading the published consultation and final documents, there will be many that question whether the new curriculum will deliver the outcomes trumpeted in the headline statements.

And so, after the original spectrum of ring binders with their prescriptive programmes of study (1980s), after the National Strategies with their lunch boxes laden with recipes for success (1990s and 2000s), after the voluminous reviews of Rose and Cambridge (2000s), and finally the rose-tinted rear view mirrors of coalition policy (2010+), the twenty five year circular story of the National Curriculum enters a new chapter. Will it be a chapter where the snake appears to bites its own tail again, or will it genuinely provide an essential revolution for revitalizing this country's prosperity?

In their initial response, The Curriculum Foundation says that

'*It is absolutely clear that schools will not have a curriculum which deserves this rating (World Class) simply by implementing the new framework. We all know that the curriculum is so much more than a jigsaw of subjects and schools will have to bring to bear considerable expertise if they are to meet both the deadline and appropriate quality standards.*'

Then:

'*Schools owe it to their young charges to see through the fog and design a curriculum which is both challenging and balanced.*'

There is considerable challenge here for leaders of schools, one which we must accept, and in so doing bring our educational expertise and passion to bear. The pressing task is to pose some simple questions, and respond by illustrating how as leaders we can develop touchstones to support our own systems of educational values and beliefs:

1. What do we believe is important for our children to learn?

2. How do we design a curriculum to deliver this?

Deciding what is important

First principles are important, even before the articulation of our visions and formulation of our aims; they provide the touchstones of our professional purpose around which we build the experience we call learning. We need these stones: if properly identified they will provide us with the compass and route map for our journey of curriculum development, and an anchorage in times of uncertainty, political or organisational.

So the first step is to revisit these, and it may help for us to start by taking more than a passing glance in the rear view mirrors of educational development ourselves, to go right back to basic principles and definitions. Do we all share and understand a common goal and purpose in that which we do? Do colleagues and children alike understand what we mean by learning? Does our community subscribe and contribute to our educational purpose?

Education, Education, Education

The first touchstone? Surely it has to be that word, 'education'. Are we all clear about what its meaning is? The word of course has its Latin roots in the word *educare*, as in 'to lead and draw out', as experienced by the young charges of Roman centurions as they were prepared for the uncertainty of that which lay ahead. The future continues to be uncertain for learners, and as educators it remains our duty to equip them with the essential skills, attitudes and knowledge to necessary for them to fulfil their potential. Is that not a timeless purpose, one that is unalterable by political will or policy?

And perhaps, in planning each of our school's curriculum offer, we should continue to reflect on the wise words of John Dewey, the so-called father of progressive education:

I believe that education is a process of living and not a preparation for future living. I believe that the school must represent present life – life as real and vital to the child as that which he carries on in the home, in the neighborhood, or on the play-ground. I believe that education which does not occur through forms of life, forms that are worth living for their own sake, is always a poor substitute for the genuine reality and tends to cramp and to deaden.

By their deeds you shall know them

If our purpose has always been timeless, then the curriculum as a route map has not necessarily been conducive to the long march of time, as evidenced by twenty five years of curricular chop and change. So let us once again visit the past to help us define a second touchstone.

The nineteenth century American educationalist John Franklin Bobbitt had it right when he described 'curriculum' as stemming from the Latin word for race course, referring to the course of *deeds and experiences* through which children grow to become the adults they should be, for success in society.

There persist many definitions of curriculum, uninspiring and dull for the most part, yet still the default model for too much of what happens in our schools: '*Sets of prescribed experiences needed to complete programmes of study*', or '*Instructional plan of skills, lessons, and objectives on a particular subject; may be authored by a state, textbook publisher.*'

Surely none of us as educators came into this profession to prescribe or execute, but rather to inspire achievement, accomplishment and aspiration, to be the catalysing difference in the lives of young children, and alchemists of human hope. There is something compelling and almost heroic about Bobbitt's definition. One is reminded of tapestries detailing the deeds and experiences of historical figures, knights of old, heroines of yore, tales of adventure, tales to inspire. It is within those words, deeds and experiences that the seeds of inspiration and aspiration surely lie, and that we find our second touchstone for curriculum design.

A tapestry curriculum

My life has been a tapestry of rich and royal hue, an everlasting vision of the ever changing view. Carol King

A tapestry is based on a combination of threads, the weft and the warp, both threads interwoven in a way which enables the final meaningful picture to emerge, neither more important than the other, but of little value without the relationship it holds with its partner thread. Ideally, to ensure the tapestry's strength and longevity they will be held in place by a well designed frame.

Let us explore the essential elements that build our curriculum story, and enable a tapestry to develop: a practical model for school leaders to use, and one which allows the unfolding of deeds and experiences which excite, enthuse and empower the learner.

1. *The Weft*

   According to Aim 3.1, from 2014 the NC will:

   - provide pupils with an introduction to the essential knowledge that they need to be educated citizens
   - introduce pupils to the best that has been thought and said
   - help engender an appreciation of human creativity and achievement

   Yet the new national curriculum and its programmes of study provide only part of our picture. They are the weft in our tapestry, those bodies of knowledge and understanding, reflecting major areas of human endeavour and ways of thinking. As schools we also have choice as to how much we use these threads, or draw upon those which we know serve our own school and community context with purpose and success already.

2. *The Warp*

For our model, we can think of these as being the essential skills for learning and social development. They are the longitudinal threads which stretch the full length of the tapestry's story, enabling the layers of weft to be built up with meaning and relevance. Here we have significant freedom as school leaders and educators. Rather than greet the absence of prescribed skills and attitudes within the new National Curriculum as meaning they aren't important, we should applaud the opportunity we are being given to explore those which are right for own contexts. In fact Aim 3.2 as good as tells us to do just that: 'teachers can develop exciting and stimulating lessons to promote the development of pupils' knowledge, understanding and skills.'

Is this not a permission we have always sought? So what will those warp threads look like? A great starting point for any primary school is offered by the following:

- Thinking skills
- Personal skills
- Enquiry skills
- Social skills
- Learning to learn and metacognitive skills
- Literacy skills
- Numeracy skills

These seven skill sets are not offered as an exhaustive list, but as a point for schools to begin conversations within and beyond their staffrooms as to what is needed for their distinctive local contexts, bearing in mind that the most vibrant curriculum offer has local, national and international dimensions.

3. *Designing The Frame*

If we want our learners' experiences and deeds in turn to develop their aspirations, then we need to ensure that children are imbued with learning and a set of life values that will equip them with the attitudes needed for the journey. Many schools are well used to reviewing such values or attributes collaboratively with their communities, and whilst there is no definitive list, the following offers a starting point for schools in their discussions.

We want children to be

- Enterprising
- Adaptable
- Compassionate

- Resilient

- Creative

A strong set of learning values not only empowers the learner. They serve as a further touchstone for school leaders, to return to as we view and review the emerging picture of the deeds and experiences of our children and young people.

4. *Telling The Tale*

What then will be the deeds of achievement and memorable experiences of the learner which will illuminate the final tapestry? We need to revisit our principles and think of the individual child, for whoever enters the doors of our school, there must be experiences which polish their strengths to accomplishment, and support their weaknesses in equal measure. We have the elements in place for our curriculum: the knowledge, skills, attitudes and values. Yet the final picture is incomplete.

It is now up to us as educators to be creative and inventive with what we know about our school context and weave those elements together in a way that allows the learner to do the deeds by which they will become known, and live the experiences which shape their lives.

In the end, the effectiveness of any national curriculum has always and will always depend upon what happens during the day-to-day commerce of the classroom. Imagine a series of events across the school calendar year which weaves together *creativity, social enterprise and basic skills*, led and run for the wider community by the children who live within it, with astute light-touch adult guidance.

- For example, what better way to inspire writers of the future than for children to organise their own Literature Festival, organising performances and workshops, presented by professionals and children, marshalling the publicity and marketing machine that delivers the final programme.

- Or maybe we turn our school hall into a museum for the community, complete with gift shop and cafe, devised and run by children.

- Or pupils establish a school garden centre, advised by local business and stocked with plants and knick-knacks grown and made by the children.

- Or an outdoor classroom where the children teach their parents or younger siblings the skills of leadership through trust exercises.

These are proven and powerful events, eminently possible in all primary schools.

The possibilities for real-life, purposeful learning – exciting and inspiring – remain with us as we shape the new curriculum, and the responsibility for teachers and Headteachers leading its development has never been greater. In the words of Shakespeare from *Measure For Measure:*

Heaven doth with us as we with torches do,
Not light them for themselves; for if our virtues
Did not go forth of us, 'twere all alike
As if we had them not.

References

1.   The Curriculum Foundation, www.curriculumfoundation.org

Wider reading

Built To Last, Jim Collins

Mindset, Carol Dweck

Unjust Rewards, Polly Toynbee

Tipping Point, Malcolm Gladwell

Ithaca, Constantine Cavafy

Chapter 15

Creating independent learners: an art or a science?

Jane Ratcliffe

The curriculum is a complicated beast. It ranges far beyond the statutory requirements of the volume that sits on our shelves into everything which the children experience while they are in our care. It is the curriculum that has to prepare children for their lives beyond school. And therefore it is the knowledge, skills, qualities and attributes that will take them through life which must be considered when a curriculum is designed. Politicians alone do not have the answer. Schools can lead and must be free to design a curriculum which really does prepare children for an uncertain future.

So the challenge is to create a whole curriculum which gives children the skills and knowledge they need, one which leaves them hungry for learning, and capable as learners – independent learners ready to shape their own future.

A: The art of irresistible learning

Values and core principles

We should start with our values. If they really underpin all our decisions then we need to start using them to shape the curriculum we teach. How can we talk about 'freedom' if we don't give children that very opportunity to explore the things that they want to learn about? How can we talk about 'quality' if we knowingly feed the children a diet of dull and unrelated lessons? How can we talk about 'happiness' if we create the perfect conditions for disengagement?

It is then the principles which sit behind a curriculum that, together with the highest quality teaching, transform learning into something real and lifelong: principles that are based on a solid philosophy of learning and on deeply rooted values. Independent learners are the result of principles that are shared and understood by the whole school community. Curriculum principles drawn up by staff and governors, and reviewed regularly, will ensure that we keep our eye on the learning ball. It is deep understanding and therefore consistency of principles that create the illusion of the effortless craft – not effortless at all, but the result of a skilled and intricately designed process.

So what are these principles which ensure we get to the place where our children become more independent, not less, during their seven years of primary schooling? These are some which might make up a school's manifesto.

There are more, and they need to be hotly debated in staffrooms to help shape curriculum planning.

Children deserve a curriculum which:

- is fun, engaging and challenges all children
- equips children to 'know what to do when they don't know what to do'
- has wow factor and a 'hook and grab'
- includes high quality texts to read
- leads to a quality product that can be shared with others
- provides diverse opportunities for reading, writing, speaking, mathematics and ICT
- is broad, balanced and based on a carefully planned skills progression
- gives children choice and is well differentiated – not merely by outcome
- provides problem solving challenges: maths and statistics, social and environmental problems, ethical and medical dilemmas
- has real, hand-on experiences and maximises opportunities for outdoor learning
- harnesses resources and expertise beyond the school.

Memory making

The art of creating independent learners lies in drawing them into their learning – we need to make learning so irresistible that the children cannot help but learn. How do we do that in an age of every increasing prescription? We do it by standing by what we believe – that is that learning must be interlinked, real and relevant. Children need to know what they are learning and why, and they need to be enthralled by it too. They must be drawn in from minute one with a wow or a hook which grabs them imperceptibly. They should build towards something real – learning with a product in mind – that has a real audience and a real importance.

Never again do I want to ask a child (or, heaven forbid, a teacher) why they are learning something, only to be told 'I don't know'.

My philosophy of primary education is a simple one; imagine, if you will, a circular room. On the floor are the basics – the stuff we must teach our children: literacy, numeracy, social understanding, technological understanding and awareness – the absolute core of what we do. Around the walls are countless doors, each one opening onto an area of life. Our job is to give the children the skills they need and to open as many doors as we can. We need to show them the joy that lies through each one, the infinite variety of human experience, and the limitless options that are available to them as they journey through life.

The previous approach to the curriculum has to go: dull, dry topics written by people who live far away from local communities, with little basis in deep underlying values and principles. We need to create topics (and borrow some that we have seen elsewhere) that excite the staff, that get them buzzing with the opportunities they could create for their children. The inspired adult becomes the inspirational teacher. The inspirational teacher weaves magic.

So topics that are real, exciting and sometimes yes, a bit naughty are created. Topics should allow children to make real choices – about the product, about the process and about the content; but topics should always take heed of the floor of my learning room – those non-negotiable skills at the heart of a lifelong learner. Our school's list of topics which allow us to extend and support children physically and intellectually, and to get children of different abilities learning from each other includes:

- Eureka! (Inventions galore with Wallace and Gromit)
- Chocaholics (A dream journey to explore the history of confection – recipes, letters, maps abound. Discussions of food miles can be heard from the clusters of hard working Heads.)
- *The Tempest* (Shakespeare's story is a gift to the primary curriculum. It's more about what won't fit in than what will.)
- What a load of rubbish (Helps us develop citizens of the future – you too can have a plastic bottle greenhouse on your playground.)
- *Dragons' Den* meets *The Apprentice* (Where else does maths become so real, so exciting, and so important? The perfect topic for collaborative group work.)

All these require are teachers who understand the principles of great learning and Headteachers who give staff the permission to fly.

B: The science behind irresistible learning

But the craft of the magic weaver is not effortless after all. For the imagination to take flight we, as Headteachers, must ensure that systems are in place to release great teaching. This is the 'science' as opposed to the 'art'.

The non-negotiables

So what is the science of teaching? This is the skills and knowledge of the teacher which enables every child to achieve their very best. The mantra 'Teach them what they don't know' is the starting point for learning that is based absolutely on the needs of each and every child. It is the ability of the teacher to design lessons which ensure every child is engaged in something that is relevant to them, be it a skill they need to learn or an activity that is needed to complete an agreed learning outcome. It is the ability of the teacher to ensure that his or her own time in the classroom is spent to maximum effect –

motivating children by a highly personalised approach to learning. This is the art of the possible and it relies on, and creates independent learners.

For example, while the teacher is engaged in highly focused group support, other children are working independently, making their own choices and using the wide range of resources that are available to them. Computers in class (not in a remote ICT suite where they are only ever used under teacher direction), mobile technology such as iPads and video cameras, and the spaces around school which are outside of class – all are used preciously to give children responsibility for their learning, and the ability to learn 'what to do when they don't know what to do'.

Independent learners understand themselves as learners; therefore the systems we use for feedback are an essential component of any successful curriculum. For too long teachers have held onto children's learning as knowledge not to be shared. But it is the children's learning and they are the ones who need to understand it. Clear and consistent marking and feedback; routines and success criteria which enable children to be their own markers; and an ongoing debate of what helps or hinders learning – each contributes to a great learner's curriculum. These are the non-negotiables – the things that have to be done, and done exceptionally well.

Beyond the classroom

Everything I have written has been based around an understanding that we are educating children for an independent life, and so surely the curriculum must reflect the life that goes on beyond the classroom. We must work hard to ensure that these rich opportunities are widely available, and this part of the curriculum must be as carefully planned as class-based learning. That's not to say it has to look the same in each school or each year, but the principles must never change: that is to give children opportunities and experiences that will stay memorably with them and will prepare them for more of the uncertainties that lie ahead. Among these I include:

- Learning in nature through Forest School activities helps develop an understanding of managing everyday risk.
- High quality residentials teach children to be independent of their parents.
- Great day-trips afford children safe opportunities to explore other environments and bring back experiences and artefacts to reflect on in class.
- Well planned and run clubs can open doors to the passions of tutors/ volunteers from the local community, from jazz and knitting to running and cooking.

Beyond the classroom, there is of course the subject of homework. Homework can be a great divider (of pupils, teachers and parents) in many primary schools; it is rarely possible to please all of the people all of the time. However, when designing a homework policy it is important to return to those guiding principles and values which operate in your classrooms: any homework must meet these and be designed to create independent learners.

No worksheets at school? Then no worksheets must go home. Children's choice matters? Then children should be allowed to choose the work they do at home. Exciting and real? Let them cook, visit museums and write self-study projects. Builds required skills? Include some expectations *personalised* to individuals. The point is that homework should teach children three things:

1. Learning doesn't just happen at school.
2. Learning is fun and collaborative.
3. We can learn about the things that interest us.

If your principles are sound and your communication is good, then the homework divide should narrow. A little at least!

The curriculum we provide is crucial in creating children who are well equipped for their life ahead: independent, skilled and principled young people who understand their skills and gifts, and are able to make decisions based on a clear understanding of who they are and what they understand. The curriculum we choose for our children could very well keep doors closed to a great many children; it is our job to weave art and science together so we open as many doors onto an exciting future as we can.

Wider reading

Brave Heads – How to lead a school without selling your soul, David Harris

Thinking Allowed on Schooling, Mick Waters

The Element: How finding your passion changes everything, Sir Ken Robinson

The World's Wife, Carol Ann Duffy

Chapter 16

Why reading and writing are fundamental

Kate Dethridge

'*A reader lives a thousand lives before he dies. The man who never reads lives only one.*' **George R.R. Martin**

Every year somewhere close to 20% of our 11-year-olds go on to secondary school with reading skills that will not allow them to access the secondary curriculum, a 'secret garden' to which they might never have access. It is only right that both the Secretary of State and Ofsted have given the acquisition of early literacy skills the highest priority in order to tackle this chronic under performance. If we can get this right by the end of primary education, children's prospects at age 16 and beyond are hugely improved.

In 2005, Sir Jim Rose developed a model of 'The Simple View of Reading'. In this, two skills need to be mastered by children in order to become fluent readers. The first is *word recognition or decoding*. The present drive on delivering a synthetic phonic programme seeks to address this. However, it is not enough in itself. The second skill required is the development of *comprehension skills*, both written and spoken. Children have to be good at both in order to become fluent readers and you can't have one without the other.

These skills need to be taught to children throughout their primary years and not just at the start. Whilst teachers in Key Stage 1 can support children in basic skills, these must be built upon in Key Stage 2. Gone are the days that the responsibility for the teaching of reading and writing lay with those who teach younger pupils. For schools to ensure that all pupils read well by the time they leave Year 6, they need to consider the following questions at the heart of any curriculum planning:

- Is there clear agreement about what children need to learn in order to be successful readers?

- What steps are school leaders taking in order to ensure consistency in the teaching of reading?

- Is there rigorous assessment of every child; in particular to identify difficulties early on in order to establish well matched and timely support?

- How do we ensure that teachers have a good knowledge of the types of book that might appeal to those in their care, for example the reluctant boy reader?

- Are systems in place to audit the reading menu of our children to ensure that they are exposed to a range of texts?

It is vitally important that children have quality stories read to them so that they become familiar with different patterns of language and have exposure to more sophisticated vocabulary and themes.

The poet Michael Rosen offers a twenty point plan that illustrates what he calls a 'book loving school' (http://www.readingrevolution.co.uk/). It's worth a read as it offers suggestions to those who work in schools about the sorts of activities and resources that should be employed to engender a love of reading not only amongst children, but within families too.

It is in everyone's best interests to ensure that all children learn to love reading. Is it a coincidence that many children who misbehave are also struggling readers? Are children with behaviour difficulties inherently poor readers or do some children use poor behaviour as a distraction from their struggle to read?

'Treat people as if they were what they ought to be and you help them become what they are capable of becoming'. Goethe

Teaching children to become powerful writers builds confidence and gives a child their voice. Both the teacher and the child have to believe that it is possible for anyone to be a writer with something worthwhile to say. How do we develop children as writers? Teachers must model writing, encourage children to 'steal' phrases and ideas they have read to use in their own work, and offer a scaffold on which pupils can begin to build their own work.

With recognition of their success, a deepening understanding of what high quality writing looks like, and a knowledge of the small steps they need to take to improve, any child can become a competent writer. Teachers need to understand the link between talking, reading and writing. Talking is of vital importance to support writing, as the work of Ros Wilson (1) testifies, and no child can write well if they are not fluent readers who read widely. By understanding this link, teachers are able to give their pupils the gift of expression: a lifelong skill and fundamental requirement of being a well-rounded adult.

Boys' underachievement in writing still exposes the greatest gap between boys and girls achievement in schools. Glancing along the shelves of any well stocked library it is clear that there is no lack of male literary talent. Nor has there ever been. Why is it then that so many boys currently seem to fail at this in our primary schools? In too many schools, there exists the 'perfect storm' in which boys have low self esteem, a lack of experience to call upon (real or imagined) and, due to a shallow diet of mainly non-fiction reading, a weak understanding of how fiction works. They don't know where to start and so switch off.

In the best schools, however, teachers plug these gaps to enable all children to become writers. If a child lacks experience to draw upon, they are taken out of school to gain experiences. If they only read non-fiction, someone audits their reading diet and ensures they are exposed to a variety of books and begin to gain an understanding of the composition of a genre . If a child lacks the vocabulary to express themselves, they collect it from books, adults and peers. Alongside this, a curriculum is planned which allows boys easy access to novels that resonate with them. In this way, even the most reluctant writer will find his voice.

'A good teacher must be able to put himself in the place of those who find learning hard.' Eliphas Levi

Even after the laudable drive for improvements in literacy that successive governments have funded, there are still children who slip through the net because they are not taught to read or write properly. This isn't about slavishly following a scheme or strategy. That will get children so far .To become a real reader or author, children need to be inspired. They need to have passion demonstrated to them and given access to worlds and experiences beyond their own. This comes from skilled, well informed and enthusiastic teachers.

As leaders, are we doing enough to train teachers in the skills they need, to develop their vision of outstanding practice in primary schools? Excellent teaching is developed through reflecting on one's own practice and that of those who are better than us. The best schools and teachers are restless for improvement, constantly asking 'what more can we do' and 'what can we do better'? Do schools spend enough time developing an understanding of excellence? Schools are currently reforming their Performance Management systems across the country. Senior leaders need to seize this opportunity to review the core professional development offer for teachers in order to ensure they remain fresh, enthused and equipped with the skills and vision to deliver excellent outcomes for pupils, particularly in relation to purposeful reading and writing across the curriculum.

Those of us who are privileged to work in schools have a duty, a moral imperative, to ensure that all children, regardless of their background, become fluent readers whose voice and opinions are heard through effective written communication. We need to get it right for the children we serve. The stakes are high; not only in terms of what happens to the life chances of those we fail, but also in terms of our accountability as centres of learning.

We hear endlessly from politicians and business leaders about the need for children to acquire the 'basics' of reading and writing as this will make them employable in years to come. But mastery of these skills offers so much more than the promise of future employment. Both reading and writing feed the soul. They allow children to experience a world beyond their own, and the path to this world is built by the teacher.

'I'm not a teacher: only a fellow traveller of whom you asked the way.'
G.B. Shaw

Teachers have an obligation to engender children with a love of reading and writing. They do this through the delivery of an appropriate, inspiring curriculum. A new National Curriculum is being introduced and schools can see it either as a constraint or an opportunity for innovation. The best practitioners will do what they have always done. They will take the document and make it their own. They will reflect, adapt and re-write until it becomes something that they are inspired to teach and that they know will capture the imagination and enthusiasm of their pupils.

School leaders must allow teachers the freedom to make changes to the curriculum and play to their strengths and interests. Best practice also dictates that there are planned opportunities for children to use and apply their literacy skills across the curriculum and not just in English lessons. Time invested by staff in making curriculum links and developing purposeful opportunities to read, discuss and write across subjects will pay huge dividends, both for the children and the teacher delivering the lessons.

If we reflect on those times when we have witnessed excellent teaching, those moments that send a tingle down the spine, they have never involved the delivery of a lesson from a scheme or handbook. They have been lessons planned following a careful assessment of the pupils' needs and experiences, based on something about which the teacher has real knowledge and an enthusiasm. They are exciting, a bit different and leave those present wanting more.

'I never teach my pupils, I only attempt to provide the conditions in which they can learn.' **Albert Einstein**

Perhaps the most important role for senior leaders in primary schools then is to provide the conditions in which children can learn. This means reviewing both the way we teach and what we teach. We must invest time in learning from the best both nationally and internationally, raise our expectations of what children in primary schools are capable of, and ensure that we deliver a curriculum that is relevant, exciting and leads to improved outcomes for our children.

If some schools, working under very difficult circumstances, are able to produce children who read fluently and write with style and skill, it must surely be possible that all schools can achieve this? Whilst each success story is unique in many ways, there are some patterns to success worth considering:

- All successful schools challenge long held orthodoxies regarding how children learn and when.
- They respond to their community and create a curriculum that is both exciting and relevant.

- They are restless in their pursuit of success, constantly looking to improve and refine what they do.
- They have high expectations of themselves and their pupils. They do not see background as a reason for under-achievement.
- Children are well known and well supported.
- Impact is measured regularly, and there is flexibility which allows for rapid revision when things are deemed less successful.

Any school's core purpose is to ensure that children are taught to read and write well. Invest time in creating a stimulating curriculum, delivered by a skilled and determined staff who have been given a vision of excellence, and children will soar.

References

1.   Big Writing: Writing Voice and Basic Skills. Oxford 2012, Ros Wilson

Wider reading

To Kill a Mockingbird, Harper Lee

Kensuke's Kingdom, Michael Morpurgo

What's the Point of School? Rediscovering the Heart of Education, Guy Claxton

Journey to Jo'burg, Beverley Naidoo

Blink: The Power of Thinking without Thinking, Malcolm Gladwell

Chapter 17

Mathematics, security and simplicity

Kate Frood

There's a word that is now creeping into the world of assessment, league tables and ministerial pronouncements: secure. Schools are now to be judged on the number of children who reach *secure* (sure, certain, assured) levels in reading writing and maths when they leave primary school represented by a 4B+. And this against the backcloth that National Curriculum levels as we know them are to be phased out.

Rather than sigh and moan about higher expectations, we must seize this word. Metaphors of 'foundations', 'pillars' and 'fragility' shape how we as professionals at our school talk about learning and teaching.

The four pillars of mathematics

Ask any experienced Year 6 teacher what they think makes for a secure mathematician leaving primary school and they will say 'they're really good mentally, they have a mental map of numbers and their relative size, they totally get place value, they can double and halve anything, they are confident with problem solving and most importantly they know their times tables inside out – oh, and they love maths.' No mention of Roman numerals, rotational symmetry or ratio. In my recent unscientific poll of Year 7 maths teachers at our local comprehensive they said virtually the same with glazed eyes and a wistful sigh.

And then that same primary teacher moves back to following 'the plan' as prescribed by their scheme, too often moving children on to the next topic before they are… *secure*.

The new mathematics national curriculum planned for introduction in September 2014 will be fine if teachers make the right choices, about what really matters, what to 'go to the wall for'. Tracking back from that eleven year old *secure* mathematician, consider what a seven year old *secure* mathematician looks like: they really know their number bonds to 10 and can apply this to pairs of numbers up to 100; they know their 2, 5 and 10 times table, they get place value to 1000, can double and half, talks about their maths – and love maths. Track back to a five year old – they can subitise the total of two dice, can order 1-20, know what they need to roll to win, know number bonds to 10 - and love maths… and it all becomes clear.

To create *secure* mathematicians is all about consistent practice from nursery and a real clarity about what really matters. We talk about four 'pillars of mathematics' in our school and concentrate our teaching time on these aspects, focusing on mental calculation, carefully planned progression within each pillar, games, fun and talk. The four pillars are:

- Place value
- Fast and secure recall of core number facts
- Visuals, images and models
- Doubling and halving.

As something of a Luddite I can see how interactive whiteboards have adversely affected that progression in visuals, images and models. It's no use having a technicolour interactive 100 square on your whiteboard ... if it's turned off. Or an image of 6 cubes plus 4 cubes, if they can't be picked up. Some ill-informed critics scorn educational theory and seek to reduce academic input into teaching training, but understanding Piaget's stages of cognitive development, particularly concrete to formal, is essential. As a profession we need to be secure in our theories of how children learn best.

As ever, the Foundation Stage have got it right with the brilliant new characteristics of learning which must be a strong thread from 3-11 too, to create those resilient learners – creative thinking, critical thinking, active learning. Our school now uses these to assess and describe all our children within end of year reports.

Too much end of Key Stage 2 achievement is fragile, dare I say insecure, precipitated by 'kill drill and skill' in Year 6; too much pupil premium money goes into Year 6 with extra staff and resources. Our goal, our measure of success is to become a 'booster free school' by 2014 because there will be no need to fill gaps, because our Year 6 pupils will have had consistently good teaching leading to secure levels of achievement. And we are nearly there.

Security

But to be secure (without anxiety, affording safety), leaving primary school is so much more than academic levels: it is about being emotionally resilient, knowing that you are fascinated by learning and the world around you, having a family and friends around you who understand your strengths and needs, and having a real sense of who you are and might be.

Being confident as a school leader about this dimension makes it easier to create the kind of curriculum that both produces secure academic levels *and* secure children. Creating a growth mindset culture, as conceived by Carol Dweck, goes a long way to creating learners (and teachers) who know how to learn from mistakes, the importance of perseverance and of taking risks. 'Good mistake!' is a seam running right through our school, uttered in just about every lesson.

So what does a secure school look like? It has a Headteacher who relentlessly returns to a simple, core and commonly shared pedagogy and vision made real in all aspects of school life. She protects staff children and parent from huge swings in thinking, policy and demands and consistently returns to that mantra. Parents love it when they feel secure (in safe keeping) leaving their children in capable hands, in a school that knows itself and is confident.

I love Tim Brighouse's brilliant *Jigsaw of a Successful School*, a short accessible read detailing how successful schools have six corner pieces (*eg* 'we sing from the same song sheet'; 'we try to do things right', 'the school is a beautiful place'), straight edges and wiggly bits. As Headteacher, you need to be clear about those corner pieces as they are what holds the jigsaw/school together; they are what makes it secure. And the curriculum is at the heart of this jigsaw.

Simplicity

A brilliant left field book is *Better* by surgeon-writer Atul Gawande. It comprises a series of essays which illustrate facets of improving medical care – hence the title of the collection. He describes brilliantly for example, how hospital death rates were dramatically reduced simply by insisting on a rigorous hand-washing regime. He has three key principles (corner pieces?) which are easily extrapolated into leadership for school improvement and curriculum planning:

- Do right
- Be ingenious
- Be diligent.

These three principles lie at the core of our school's practices. We won't go as far as coffee cup slogans but again and again, when making decisions we find ourselves quoting these three simple principles to each other, whether it's how to respond to the new curriculum, tackling the child who just won't engage with learning, casting a play or planning a complicated route to a museum. We are all empowered by having this simple reference point; it makes us feel secure.

As a profession we are sometimes rather guilty of making a meal of things... over detailed planning, endless policies, too many meetings, too defensive a response to politicians. Schools spend a lot of time writing vision statements by committee, struggling to re-invent wheels of grandiose phrases about citizenship, enlightenment, global awareness, inclusion and equal opportunity. Many of these statements then sit in a file, rarely referred to.

A breakthrough for us in curriculum planning was declaring that our core purpose was simply to teach the children to read, write and do maths brilliantly, and to ensure that they developed 'a love of learning and a desire to go on learning'. Once this was clearly communicated, our job was to decide on the vehicle, the culture, the pedagogy to make that happen. As the brothers Heath argue in *Switch*, it is simple methods that yield the most extraordinary results. Their three principles for change are: 'direct the rider, motivate the elephant and shape the path'.

What shapes our school in our core purpose of securing high levels for all in reading writing and maths is then creating a curriculum which has:

- Collective curiosity and imagination;
- Positive memorable experiences;
- Authentic outcomes
- Access to social and cultural capital for all.

Combined, these principles create children who love learning and who have a sense that there is more to discover out there and that they have the skills – and the right – to access it.

Our teachers work from a loose curriculum overview detailing what they must cover each year, creating three separate, engaging term-long topics. Their focus must then be on:

- Teaching just above what the child can already do, applying Vygotsky's brilliant Zone of Proximal Development or ZPD
- Purposeful practice of the new learning
- Creating a growth mindset culture
- Quality relationships – high quality interactions and conversations particularly around next steps for learning, with time of course for interesting digressions
- The timing of these adult/child interventions…..knowing when to intervene
- Helping a child be ready for the next step by doing what is right for them now (we do not exist as primary schools simply to prepare for secondary education).

All these key aspects help the children to be secure in their ability to learn, and help teachers to be secure in knowing the next steps for each child rather than the next page of the scheme. And then as professionals, ready and secure about defending our position to any external visitor, we constantly monitor, evaluate, review and reflect from the outset.

We have a teaching assistant, in her sixties, who has worked in our school for three different Heads, countless teachers from outstanding to inadequate, and who has sat through endless training days. She always pipes up with 'It's not rocket science' as we discuss best practice: a cliché yes, but perhaps we should listen to those wise words and be more confident to do what we know is right.

As a new set of curriculum changes arrives, it seems critical to hang on to a simple core pedagogy: to take time as a school leader and with staff to really determine what shapes how you teach, why you teach, and what really matters – to set your corner pieces. Only then can we start to develop that consistency and create those secure learners we are ambitious to see.

Wider reading

Better, Atul Gawande

The Jigsaw of a Successful School, Tim Brighouse

Mindset, Carol Dweck

Switch, Chip and Dan Heath

Mind in Society, Lev Vygotsky

Chapter 18

A culture of mathematical thinking

Pamela Matty

It is always illuminating when talking to primary teachers about their philosophy of teaching mathematics.

Discussions vary on a spectrum: from teachers who have a very clear approach to developing pupils as mathematicians in their school, to teachers who are much less certain, with a reserved response which can include sharing a lack of confidence in their own abilities as mathematicians. The chasm between views can range from developing mathematical thinkers who are empowered by the National Curriculum, with a limitless view of what pupils can potentially achieve, to a slavish following of the minimum requirements with pupils being limited by an expectation that all will achieve just an average level.

Where teaching maths becomes exciting is when the teaching force in the school has a clear whole-school approach. When mathematical talk is developed, pupils engage with abstract concepts, logic is encouraged through connections and trial and error. Pupils work on open ended problems and make sense of their real world through mathematical experiences. The curriculum content then becomes the fundamentals of a programme to engage pupils in a personalized mathematical journey.

Let me explore this in more detail at one large primary school in the heart of Birmingham, where pupils explore specialising, generalizing and conjecturing as mathematicians, where *maths talk* is central to the teaching of mathematics. An early lesson for new teachers who join the school is the art and language of being able to articulate your mathematical ideas to others. The school is unusual in that at the age of ten or eleven, more able pupils take their GCSE maths with highly successful results over the past two decades. This is a school where there is no limit put on mathematical achievements.

What then are the key elements of mathematics teaching in this school? They are three-fold:

1. A philosophy of teaching maths
2. Professionally developing the team of staff to lead maths teaching in their classes
3. Creating a culture of all pupils being successful mathematical thinkers.

1 A philosophy of teaching mathematics

In 1982 The Cockcroft Report referred to a 'Handbook of suggestions for teachers', published in 1937, which advised teachers to teach maths through practical experiences and discussion:

> *First, by way of introduction, should come practical and oral work designed to give meaning to, and create interest in, the new arithmetical conception – through deriving it from the child's own experience – and to give him confidence in dealing with it by first establishing in his mind correct notations of the numerical and quantitative relations involved in the operation.[1]*

Cockcroft (1982) explored this further by recommending that:

> *The primary mathematics curriculum should enrich children's aesthetic and linguistic experience, provide them with the means of exploring their environment and develop their powers of logical thought, in addition to equipping them with the numerical skills which will be a powerful tool for later work and study.[2]* (Paragraph 287)

The philosophy articulated here is that pupils at all levels develop the language of mathematics: they think through their maths problems, articulate their ideas, make connections, and thus mathematical relationships are developed through active problem solving throughout the school.

Walking around our culturally diverse and animated school you will hear teachers talking regularly about maths with their colleagues. Teachers, support staff and pupils engage in active learning walks looking at maths in their classrooms, on the playground, in corridors or dining rooms. The culture of being a mathematician permeates the school. Interestingly, the Board of Education's advice on teaching maths from 1937 was reiterated in Ofsted's excellent report in 2011 on Good practice in primary mathematics:

> *Practical, hands-on experiences of using, comparing and calculating with numbers and quantities and the development of mental methods are of crucial importance in establishing the best mathematical start in the Early Years Foundation Stage and Key Stage 1. The schools visited couple this with plenty of opportunities for developing mathematical language so that pupils learn to express their thinking using the correct vocabulary.[3]*

Maths is in our everyday lives, whether our students are thinking of a career in natural science, engineering, gardening, medicine, finance or catering; it's a key part of all of these and many more vocations and professions. Real life maths in classrooms comes alive when teachers create *real and realistic* problems for pupils to solve, involve pupils in planning educational visits through costings and time plans, use ratio in their food technology lessons, explore a range of data handling through science and geography.

Equally vital is developing the stamina of mental maths agility as a core element for any child to succeed as a mathematician. And all staff in a school being consistent and persistent with mental maths which really challenges pupils, at pace and with fun!

It's very interesting to look at the games played in a school, and how they develop over the years. A good example is the game of input and output, sometimes known as the function machine game. In the Early Years this can be a magic box where a small object is put in and a large object is pulled out, or one toy is put in and two are pulled out. As you move through school this 'game' will evolve into a much more complex formula involving squared numbers, divisions and a multiplicity of operations which will be recorded as an algebraic expression by the child leading the game. This is one of many examples of how schools have core mental games they use all the way through school.

Talking together as professionals about the mental maths strategies to be taught, the methods to teach times tables, and how best to introduce symbols to pupils through games – each is part of a school's culture of being innovative, being consistent, and sharing good practice.

It seems so obvious that where a school has a clear philosophy on the teaching of maths, and the commitment to developing the workforce professionally to deliver high quality mathematical experiences, pupils will succeed; but how regularly in the past few years have teachers joined a staff meeting where the underlying principles or philosophy of teaching of maths in the school have been discussed? School leaders need to make time for this intellectual exploration of maths.

2 Professionally developing the team of staff to lead maths teaching in their classes

Consider the following questions in relation to the professional development of staff in our schools:

a. What priority does a school place on the mathematical qualifications of staff they employ?

b. In the interview process, what opportunity does the candidate have to show their mathematical thinking?

c. Once employed, how do new teachers and teaching assistants receive training on the school's approach to the teaching of maths?

d. What priority does maths have in the cycle of staff development within the school?

e. What place does maths have in the performance management of all staff in the school?

f. How effective is the moderation of maths in developing discussions about the teaching of maths with staff and with children in the school?

In our school, maths subject expertise and interest is a key criterion for short-listing teachers. As part of the interview process, our pupils engage candidates in a mental maths quiz. Once employed, all new teachers and support staff work with the maths leader on an induction programme. The induction programme is focused on (a) training on the philosophy of maths teaching in the school and (b) working alongside lead teachers on a team teaching programme to immerse new colleagues in the world of maths in the school.

Maths has a high priority on the whole-school and individual staff members' professional development schedules, which includes a half termly moderation of maths with individual teachers talking about the progress of each child's mathematical development. The whole system of professional development is designed to share inspirational practice whilst building the confidence and skills of those at an earlier stage of development as a teacher of maths.

Developing new curricular programmes is always exciting. Starting with the national requirements, and then using the most creative tools at our disposal – the knowledge and experience of our teachers. The maths leader involves the teaching team in mapping out a journey through each of the key areas of maths. This allows for continuity between teachers, and pupils are monitored carefully to ensure that each year they move forward from their own starting points; there is precious little chance that any child will be left behind. Parents and pupils all have copies of their child's learning journey in maths as they move through the school. This creates a shared common experience involving families in active learning.

Time for staff to share innovative ideas will further develop a depth of understanding in maths:

- teachers being willing to ask for help in topics and subject content in which they feel less confident
- planning maths challenges together, then reflecting on how each group of learners responded
- reviewing one another's class exercise books to share pupil progress, thereby developing an understanding of the curriculum
- as a new curriculum is developed, taking a thread of the curriculum and studying how teachers in different year groups have developed investigations in this area
- sharing through pupil discussions what the pupils particularly enjoy in the curriculum and how they think it could be even better.

In a recent CBI report, First Steps, the researchers called for a new approach for schools, recommending:

Teachers are the key – we need to end the culture of micro-management and treat them as professionals. The role of good teaching cannot be overstated. During the period of just one year, pupils with a very effective maths teacher gain 40% more learning than those with a poorly performing one. Importantly, the effects are especially significant for young people from disadvantaged backgrounds. (4)

A professional utopia would be for school leaders and maths subject specialists to spend time with all our colleagues in their classrooms, to observe maths being taught, jointly teach lessons, and to evaluate pupil outcomes together. We can approach this ideal if we prioritise this style of professional development. By creating an open door culture in school where staff work together on maths lessons, the potential talent pool of all the staff is unlocked and shared.

I imagine the old elephant and bun investigation, where the challenge is to move the elephant through a number of rooms collecting as many buns as possible in the shortest number of moves. The challenge in school is to provide skilled, innovative teachers with the opportunity to share their practice, and to provide time for those who are developing to observe and work alongside others to perfect their craft of teaching mathematics. In the elephant and bun investigation there are many different ways to move through the rooms, the important element being that the treasure in each room has been collected as you move through.

Much has been written about effective and outstanding leadership: leading maths requires a passion for the subject, and the well-educated, enquiring mind of a professional who enjoys a mathematical challenge. It requires an ability to examine the demands of a prescribed programme of study and tailor it to a particular school population's needs. Further, it requires a culture of promoting the mathematical abilities of all staff who work with children, providing the space and time to draw upon their strengths and develop those who are less confident.

Today's schools are data rich; we can compare within and beyond the school. The wise school uses a balance of comparative data within the school, knowing where each child is and identifying the support and extension for particular pupils. Equally, it is mindful of taking opportunities to learn how other schools do things, how similar children in different contexts are accelerating in their learning.

Leaders in schools where *mathematics matters* provide high quality, bespoke induction programmes for maths as new staff join teams, with an active staff handbook for maths clarifying the 'givens' in the school. Weekly professional meetings are held for staff to review the impact of their maths teaching that week, with team leaders providing timely coaching for individual staff with a view to their moving forwards to mentor others. These schools create energy and excitement for teachers by establishing their own action research, mini projects to look at how the best of current mathematical thinking nationally and internationally can be brought to the primary classroom.

3 Creating a culture of all pupils being successful mathematical thinkers

The celebration of maths is an intrinsic part of a strong culture of maths within a school. In our Birmingham context, this takes many forms: a key Olympic value of excellence is demonstrated everyday through the celebration of mathematical achievements; there are maths awards in assemblies; there are local trails to study market stalls and visits across the city which involve maths in real life; pupils compete against their personal best in weekly mental maths agility challenges.

On an annual basis, a Maths Olympiad brings together schools from the local community in a maths challenge, each competing as a team to be the Olympic champions. There are many different challenges schools can engage in to develop a wider maths community, including the national maths association challenges.

As a mathematician, what interested you? Was it the beauty of numbers and patterns? Was it the challenge of searching for a proof through logic and deduction, or an enjoyment of shape in art and everyday life? We all have areas of maths we are drawn to. Our challenge is to provide a breadth of experience and challenge in maths from the moment pupils enter our schools. What we begin with excitement and colour in Reception needs relentless focus, fun and ambition as children move through their infant and junior years.

And primary teachers everywhere should display in their classrooms the wise words of Professor Stan Gudder (University of Denver):

The essence of mathematics is not to make simple things complicated, but to make complicated things simple.

References

1.   Board of Education Handbook of suggestions for teachers. HMSO 1937.

2.   Report of the Committee of Inquiry into the Teaching of Mathematics in Schools under the Chairmanship of Dr WH Cockcroft, HMSO 1982

3.   Good practice in primary mathematics: evidence from 20 successful schools, OFSTED, November 2011 Ref: 110140

4.   First Steps: a new approach for our schools. CBI 2012.

Wider reading

Handsworth Revolution: The Odyessy of a School, David Winkley

How Do Expert Classteachers Really Work?, Tony Eaude

Essential Pieces: The Jigsaw of a Successful School, Tim Brighouse

Inside the Black Box: raising standards through classroom assessment, Paul Black & Dylan Wiliam

Mathematical Snacks, Jon Millington

Websites

nrich.maths.org

www.nationalstemcentre.org.uk

www.m-a.org.uk

everychildcounts.edgehill.ac.uk

Chapter 19

Is there ever really a new curriculum?

Laurence Pitt

'As one gets older, one discovers that everything is going to be exactly the same with different hats on.' Mark Twain

A 'new' primary curriculum starts to see its way into schools from September 2013, ready for full implementation by September 2014. There has been lots of discussion and disagreement in staff meetings and professional gatherings throughout the land about what this will mean for teachers, pupils and school leaders: how plans will need to be drawn up, scrapped and redrawn; what resources will need to be purchased; questions raised over content versus skills – what about those dates and timelines for history?.

All this whilst remembering that through this period of change we must continue to meet the needs of all the pupils in our care every day, to ensure that potentials are realised, imaginations are stimulated and continued progress is mapped.

An exercise in managing change of any size and description is always going to be laced with degrees of difficulty and worry; we all know this. A change to the National Curriculum is a big one. After all it's national, so I guess it should come as no surprise that anxieties run deep and the uncertainty that is felt amongst the profession is real and palpable. However, we all have a full school year to play with this new thing, to test it out and mould it to the shape and texture that we want for our own schools and settings…and yet I have a sense that the anxieties are immediate and the uncertainties about how we will make this work are floating in the collective educational ether, a bit difficult to grasp hold of, like shadows that flit across the day to day of our professional lives.

So what can we do to help ourselves through this period of uncertainty and try to put some anchor points down which might allow us to start moving forward with a degree of confidence and optimism that we can actually manage this process and come out the other side smiling?

I am going to suggest two things that might help and that we will be trying to do in our setting:

Ask questions…get them right…

Firstly, take the time to formulate the right questions to ask about how the 'new' primary curriculum can be used to advantage your pupils – centre those questions on what happens already in your setting that is successful, imaginative and relevant.

Look back to look forward...

Secondly, consider what others have previously said about what a curriculum should do and how it should prepare children for the future – this might help to lay down some core principles (or just reaffirm those that exist already) to underpin the 'new' primary curriculum in your practice.

Getting the questions right

Since starting to work with Edison Learning UK (*1) eight years ago we have used the model of a primary curriculum based on core learning skills which cut across age, stage, phase and subject areas. Some of the questions that need to be asked of the new curriculum must link into these learning skills since they are at the heart of our curriculum and must be used to continue to shape how we work in the future – how we learn, how we plan, how we deliver, how we develop new materials, and how we reflect on successes and failures in what we do. So some of the questions might look like the following:

- Where are the opportunities in the new curriculum for children and adults to learn together and to learn with others? How can we first identify those opportunities and then exploit them by building on what we do well already? Can we seek out areas in the new curriculum that excite us with the potential for completely different experiences to learn together with others without worrying too much about the what, the how and the why to start with – details can be developed later. If there is excitement being generated then the details come easily at a later point.

- Are there areas in the new curriculum that are ripe for developing independence and responsibility in pupils? Might this be in one particular subject area initially? If so, which one and who is going to take on the responsibility for trialling some learning with a year group in that area and then sharing it across the school?

- If improving own learning and performance is a key skill that is valued, can we link the development of this skill to the new maths orders, say, so that the organisation of learning in mathematics makes sense in relation to our curriculum? Might this allow us to focus on the ne' curriculum as a compliment to what we offer rather than viewing it as a burden to be coped with?

- What are the opportunities in the new curriculum that will further develop our children's sense of self worth, and how can we structure these opportunities to foster greater understanding of self and others? How about looking closely at the geography and history orders to see where an appreciation of place, time and context can be used to compare our lives and the values we hold with other places, times and cultures in ways that we might not have considered before?

- For every year group, can we identify the place in the English orders that lends itself to an explicit piece of work on speaking and listening? Is there some way that we can link year-groups together cross-key stage and cross-phase so that a piece of joint speaking and listening work can be developed?

(*1) Edison Core Learning Skills

Focus Core Skill	Learning with Others	Developing Independence & Responsibility	Improving own Learning and Performance	Developing Sense of Self Worth & Understanding of Self and Others	Thinking Skills	Speaking and Listening

Looking backwards to plan forwards

There are always going to be texts which are useful to reference for making us pause and think about what we really want to achieve from a curriculum. Two texts that seem to be helpful for doing just this at the current time are:

- *2020 Vision: Report of the Teaching and Learning in 2020 Review Group*, Department for Education and Skills 2006
- *First Steps: A New Approach For Our Schools*, The Confederation of British Industry 2012

The Teaching and Learning in 2020 Review Group was tasked by the then Secretary of State for Education to report on how the education system in this country could best meet the needs of all children and prepare them for the future. In a short letter to the Secretary of State at the start of the report Christine Gilbert writes,

> We were asked to establish a clear vision of what personalised teaching and learning might look like in our schools in 2020. You identified this as a key educational priority; we agree that this is what every parent wants, what every child deserves and what the country needs if we are to meet the global challenges of the 21st century... The key challenge for the Review Group was to consider how the education system, not just individual schools, might enable learning and teaching to meet pupils' needs most effectively. Strategic action, locally and nationally, should reflect, support and extend what is already happening in this area in some schools; as we have indicated, however, it needs to do more than that. Our recommendations therefore focus on what is needed to effect systemic change.

The focal point of the report is the concept of 'personalised learning', a phrase that we don't tend to hear too much about currently but one that was certainly in vogue five years ago. Clustered around this central concept is a list of recommendations that suggest ways that a personalised learning approach would benefit the long term prospects of all pupils as they move through their formal educational career and into the world beyond.

The recommendations come under headings such as 'high quality teaching', 'designing schools for personalising learning', 'engaging parents and carers in their children's education' and 'a strategy for systemic innovation'. There is also a recommendation under the heading 'Summative Assessment and the National Curriculum' which calls for a further research group to be established to look into 'evidence for the use of curriculum flexibilities'. Whether these recommendations were taken heed of within Whitehall I'm not sure but it seems that a well respected group of educationists certainly felt that a flexible use of curriculum merited further examination – so if that was the case then, why would it not be the case now, when we are on the cusp of a new primary curriculum?

The 2020 Vision Report also spends some time considering the skills, attributes and attitudes which any curriculum and school system should place value on if the children moving through the system are going to be advantaged as they into the employment market. These often-called 'soft skills' are in my view vital for young people today:

- being able to communicate orally at a high level
- reliability, punctuality and perseverance
- knowing how to work with others in a team
- knowing how to evaluate information critically
- taking responsibility for, and being able to manage, one's own learning and developing the habits of effective learning
- knowing how to work independently without close supervision
- being confident and able to investigate problems and find solutions being resilient in the face of difficulties
- being creative, inventive, enterprising and entrepreneurial.

While at first glance they may appear as strange bedfellows, there are clear links between this particular section of the 2020 Vision Report and the CBI's 'First Steps' document. Although the initial motivation and underlying premise of the two pieces of research may be very different (2020 Vision – to establish a clear vision of what personalised teaching and learning might look like in our schools in 2020; CBI's First Steps – improving education in order to realise the enormous potential economic gain when getting it right) it seems that in their findings and recommendations there is a clear synchronicity.

Namely, that in order for the school system to best enable the young people that it serves to develop the skills, attitudes and attributes which will allow them to make the most of their futures (and, consequently, create the best future for us all) there needs to be a curriculum (in the broadest sense) that is firmly rooted in rigorous academic practice alongside the development of a clearly articulated set of skills, attributes and attitudes. In the Forward to First Steps, the CBI director general, John Cridland says,

> *In practice, this means that we must develop rigour in the curriculum and better exams, but that is only part of the solution. The other factors that make schools systems successful – like community support, good teaching and a culture and ethos that extends rigour beyond the merely academic – also need to be fostered. We set out some key steps governments can take to ensure their visions for vibrant schools are delivered. This includes defining a new performance standard based on the whole person we want to develop, and a rigorous and demanding accountability regime that assesses schools' performance on a wider basis than the narrow measure of exams.*

The new curriculum that we are facing may surely be viewed as an opportunity to move in a positive direction, to allow us to re-think how we want to deliver a curriculum. Looking afresh at familiar subject matter and encountering new content enables us to question assumptions that we may have been operating under for some time in our classroom practice and to consider the principles that underlie that practice. The Turner Prize winning artist Jeremy Deller has said that 'it's not what you make, but what you make happen' that really counts. Surely any curriculum, whether new, old or middle-aged is not what is really important, but what we make happen with it.

References

1.   www.edisonlearning.net

Wider reading

Fish! Omnibus. A Remarkable Way to Boost Morale and Improve Results, Steve Lundin, John Christensen, Harry Paul & Philip Strand

The Art of Being Brilliant, Andy Cope and Andy Whitaker

The 5 Dysfunctions of a Team – A Leadership Fable, Patrick Lencioni

Hurray for Diffendoofer Day, Dr Seuss & Jack Prelutsk

Maverick: The Success Story Behind the World's Most Unusual Workplace Ricardo Semler

Websites

okgo.net – watch any of the OK GO music videos to get an insight into the art of the possible.